PRAISE FO

"If you like to laugh, like to cry, like to be "wowed," or like to be challenged, then you're going to love this book. As Scott so masterfully writes, the words of Jesus—"It is finished"—are the words that have unlocked the code to my identity in Christ; an identity that when realized, empowers me to BE a supernatural world changer. I guarantee as you read this book you will be jumping out of your skin screaming, "Is it really this simple?" and "Why hasn't anyone ever told me this before?" *The Rhema Code* is a mind shifting and life transforming book, and if you want to really leave your "mark" on history and change the world you've got to read it. It will change your life forever!"

—Kevin Troyer, Leader, The Promise

"Scott Schang is an amazing apostolic leader whose heart has been captured by the revelation of the Kingdom. I can honestly say that I don't know anyone else who reflects the "heart of the Father" more accurately. His book, *The Rhema Code*, challenges many religious stereotypes and mindsets that have kept the Body of Christ weak and ineffectual for too long. This book will open your eyes to the reality of the finished work of Christ inside of you. These truths, when embraced, will launch you on an amazing journey of intimacy with "Papa," and into a supernatural lifestyle, with a world changing impact."

—Dan Schiopu, Teacher-Leader, The Promise

"In our world today, the attack point of the enemy (Satan) is the believer's identity. Our identity is not for sale! Scott has such a revelation of this. This book literally has an impartation of the heart of God on every page. You will feel His heart beat released like never before through these simple truths put in a way easy to digest that immediately will change the way you see yourself. A must read for all!"

—Todd White

"A MUST READ FOR 21ST CENTURY BELIEVERS"

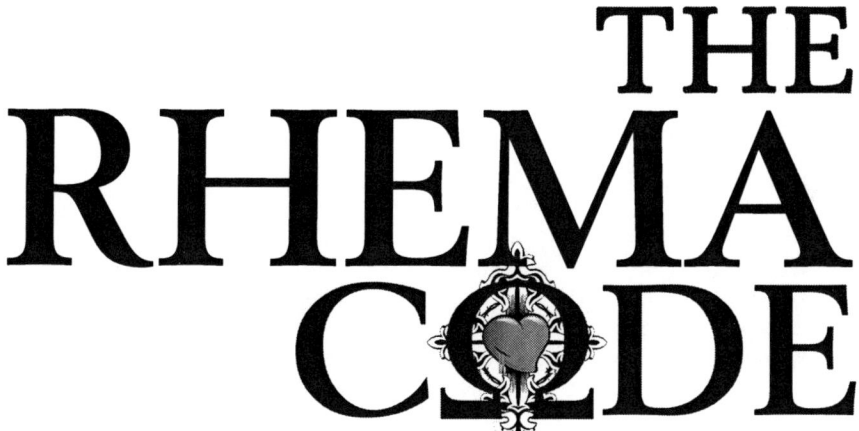

THE RHEMA CODE

Identity: The Greatest Mystery Ever Revealed...

SCOTT SCHANG

© 2010 Scott Schang

All Rights Reserved.

All right reserved. No portion of this book may be reproduced, stored in a retrieval system, or transmitted in any form or by any means—electronic, mechanical, photocopy, recording, scanning, or other—except for brief quotations in critical reviews or articles, without the prior written permission of the publisher.

All Scripture quotations, unless otherwise indicated, are taken from The New King James Version.

First published by Dog Ear Publishing
4010 W. 86th Street, Ste H
Indianapolis, IN 46268
www.dogearpublishing.net

ISBN: 978-160844-725-1

This book is printed on acid-free paper.

Printed in the United States of America

"Scripture quotations taken from the Amplified® Bible, Copyright © 1954, 1958, 1962, 1964, 1965, 1987 by The Lockman Foundation Used by permission." (www.Lockman.org)

"Scripture taken from *The Message*. Copyright © 1993, 1994, 1995, 1996, 2000, 2001, 2002. Used by permission of NavPress Publishing Group."

"Scripture taken from the New King James Version. Copyright © 1982 by Thomas Nelson, Inc. Used by permission. All rights reserved."

Scripture quotations marked NLT are taken from the Holy Bible, New Living Translation, copyright 1996, 2004. Used by permission of Tyndale House Publishers, Inc., Wheaton, Illinois 60189. All rights reserved.

For Lori

Contents

Chapter One 7

    Identity Theft

Chapter Two 21

    No Matter How It Tastes, Sounds, Feels, Smells or Looks!

Chapter Three 39

    The Next Great Move of God…You!

Chapter Four 71

    Complete

Chapter Five 105
> Faith Equals Perception

Chapter Six 121
> It is Finished

Chapter Seven 137
> A Family Culture

Chapter Eight 151
> Empowering a Power Culture

Chapter Nine 171
> The Cost of the Code

Acknowledgments

Jesus. You are so good, all the time. I love you.

Lori Schang. My one and only! You add such color and pizzazz to our journey; you make life fun. I love you.

Casey, Ashley, Laik and Rais Schang. It is such an honor for Lori and I to be in this Kingdom journey with our children and grandchildren. You are amazing and we love you.

Destiny Schang and Robbie Wilbur. As parents we couldn't be prouder of you. In choosing each other you have chosen well. In choosing Jesus you have become amazing world changers! We love you both.

Casey and Destiny. Your are both a living testimony of the goodness of God on display for the world and you make our hearts very proud. It is so honoring to have you by our side advancing God's Kingdom. Thank you for allowing life as P.K.'s. be a good thing!

Mom. Thank you for choosing Jesus and for loving me.

Kevin, Kirstin, Kaitlynn and Kristianna Troyer. Thank you for years of loyal friendship and selfless serving!

Bruce and Alyce Flanagan. Thank you for your leadership and your courage.

Dan and Alina Schiopu. What an honor it is to walk with you.

John and Chris Christopherson. Thank you for being part of our family and our team.

Jonathan and Malisa Christopherson. Thank you for pastoring so well and for being who you are.

Dave and Sandy Minor. Thank you for giving yourselves to so many over the years including Lori and me.

The Promise Staff. What a joy it is to hang out with you.

The Promise Worship Band. Thank you for all of your hard work and sacrifice of time. You are so appreciated.

Monika and Jodie. Thank you for your inspiration.

Shop Girls. Thank you for "being" amazing and fearless.

David and Debbie Lenihan. Thank you for your vision and partnering.

Kaine Thompson. Thank you for your excellent help in editing.

To my Promise Family: God has done a great job "to you, in you and through you." You are all amazing and I love you!

Foreword

Many years ago, Scott and Lori started attending our church in Longview, Washington. Shortly, the couple surrendered their life to the will and kingdom of God, and their lives were transformed. Steadily they grew in their spiritual life. About that same time they were wonderfully filled with the Holy Spirit.

It was evident that there was a "call of God" on their lives. During that same time frame, I joined both Scott and Lori in marriage. It was our joy to see them go for training at Portland Bible College in preparation for ministry.

They had a burden for their own community and felt led of God to go to a church where youth ministry was in great need. Our eldership agreed with this, sent and released them to function in youth ministry.

After college, Scott became the senior pastor of the church that today is called The Promise in Woodland, Washington. Some years ago my daughter and her family felt directed of the Lord to become a part of that church. All of the family including my two grandsons are fully engaged in ministry within The Promise.

Years ago Scott and Lori sat under my teaching on "The Kingdom of God." Today God has taken them into further revelation of the Kingdom of God. Scott has consistently and thoroughly taught on this subject and has taken it to realms of revelation beyond what I saw. That revelation is revealed in this book. It is wonderful to have sons that can learn from fathers. It is equally wonderful when the son's revelation transcends the father's. There is a biblical principle referred to as "a proceeding word" Deut 8:3 and Matt 4:4. In this book Scott demonstrates a proceeding Word.

In my opinion, this book is theologically, doctrinally, and scripturally sound. Get ready! This book will rock your world as to how you have looked at things that have been commonly taught. This book will assault much of how you have viewed salvation, our condition in Christ and the Kingdom of God. This book is not for the "faint of heart." This book has forced me to look at some of my own points of view after many years of ministry. This book is called "The Rhema Code." The Greek word "Rhema" is used to describe truth that is revelatory as opposed to didactic written truth. Revelatory truth; however, will never contradict Logos truth, the written Word of God.

Scott Schang is one of most upright men that I have had the privilege of knowing. He and his family are a model of what a Christian family should be like. I highly recommend this book to you, and pray that "The Rhema Code" will be broken to you.

David E. Minor
Pastor of Columbia Heights Assembly of God, Longview, WA (retired)

Note: For the past 20 years, Pastor David Minor has been mentoring pastors throughout Washington and Oregon.

Introduction

This very moment there is a battle waging in unseen realms over your identity. The warfare is intense and the stakes are high! If you catch the reality of who you are "in Christ" you become a dangerous weapon against the enemy of the Cross. If you don't, you remain bound to the limitations of a fallen world as a mere observer of the great drama of Heaven unfolding around you.

What was God's intention when He captured your heart and called you into His world?

> *Most assuredly, I say to you, he who believes in Me, the works that I do he will do also; and greater works than these he will do, because I go to My Father.* (John 14:12)

What did Jesus mean when He said, "greater works than these?" He is stating unequivocally that "he who believes in Me" will be endued with supernatural ability, i.e., the Holy Spirit—the Spirit of God within you.

God's intention is to have supernaturally empowered believers who know who they are as they <u>accurately represent God</u> to a lost and dying world! The battle is extreme. (Do you really want to engage in battle when you don't have faith in your equipment?) The truth is God has fully equipped you as powerful supernatural weapons!

The Rhema Code is made up of spiritual truths solidly based on the Word of God. This book is my attempt to bring to you the powerful revelation of a believer's true identity waiting to be discovered, like a rare treasure unearthed and displayed for the world to see.

"We have this treasure ---" (Voice)

Here comes God on display—and we are the showcase—the living revelation of light to a world bound by darkness; the <u>people of God, agents of Glory on assignment</u>, demonstrating the reality of a <u>superior Kingdom</u>.

Is there anything that compares to the Divine touch on a human heart; when Glory intercepts faith like the blending of precious ingredients making up <u>an amazing new creation</u>? I don't think so!

With one touch of God's fingerprint on the canvas of <u>a yielded human heart, a masterpiece is created</u>; yet easily and often undiscovered and unappreciated, missed by the undiscerning eye of natural perception and religious tradition, unable to see beyond the external, unable to see the wondrous and miraculous <u>treasure of a heart transformed by Heaven</u>. Treasure

The Rhema Code is a book about an explosive "now Word" message! It is a message given over 2000 years ago by Jesus for us to communicate around the world today; a message that carries with it certain identifying elements intended for every believer to visibly carry and display on the outside but which are birthed and nurtured on the inside.

> *His divine power has given to us all things that pertain to life and godliness, through the knowledge of Him who called us by glory and virtue, by which have been given to us exceedingly great and precious promises, that through these you may be partakers (partners) of the divine nature...* (2 Pet 1:3-4)

There is some dispute in Christian circles about the use and difference between the Greek terms "rhema" and "logos," which both mean "word" and are often used interchangeably. It is not my intent in this book to argue one side or the other. For me, the issue is settled. I define "rhema" (pronounced ray-muh) as the spoken word or the revealed word of God to His people; the now living Word, yet I want to emphasize that *rhema* is always in agreement with *logos*, the written Word. It is the "now" living application of the Word on display through believers.

I define "code" as a system of rules or guidelines that release the full value, content and meaning of a message, primarily used in the context of communication. What I am presenting here is a set of "rhema truths," the now word of revelation to believers who desire greater intimacy with Christ and the supernatural manifestations of the Spirit "gifted" to them as sons and daughters of the King.

The Rhema Code is a world changing reality—a spiritual DNA shift of endless possibilities and culture changing dynamics; an equipping and empowering of individuals with Supernatural identity and power.

When the powerful imprint of the living Word is implanted in the heart, a radical identity shift takes place forever changing and launching people into "World Changer" status. Too many of us are bound by a "performance driven" style of "churchianity" which has robbed us of our identity and the power of the Spirit. These believers often face disillusionment and cynicism, leading defeated lives, forever living from an old mindset, an old identity and an old nature.  They could have lived amazing power-filled lives had they embraced the full scope of what God has done inside of them. It breaks my heart to watch people place more power in a lie than in the truth and miss out on such an outrageous experience of living as a "Son or Daughter" of God.

When we truly embrace the full meaning of the message and carry the "Code" to its intended purpose we will witness a revolution of Kingdom advancement like never seen before as the people of God begin to live from their true identity!

In *The Rhema Code* you will find answers to questions you may never thought of or had the courage to ask. If you will embrace God's best for you as He opens the eyes of your understanding, I guarantee it will rock your world and the world around you.

Imagine the possibilities…
Experience the reality!

Note to the Reader: all scriptural references in *The Rhema Code* are from the New King James version of the Bible, unless otherwise noted. The use of the term "Rhema" in the title of this book is not in affiliation with any group, denomination or organization. And, if there seem to be repeating ideas and themes as you read through this book; read on. This is on purpose and with intent. I have found it very beneficial for people to have a look at ideas from many angles—it facilitates the removal of layers or pre-conditioned thoughts as you receive revelation or what I call "Rhemalation," the personalization of the unfolding now Word of God for each believer. Don't be overly concerned with "figuring" it all out. Let "it" soak in and set for a while. *Rhemalation* is more caught than taught and one of my pet sayings is "we want to lead people into intimation not information." I want you to have such a personal encounter with God that your intimacy level goes off the charts and revolutionizes your life.

The heart of God and the language of Heaven can be found in many media expressions around the world including Hollywood; for example, one of the great lines in the movie industry is found in the latest version of *Alice in Wonderland*. Alice is faced with the impossible task of fighting the evil dragon and breaking the dark spell over Wonderland. At this critical juncture of the story where the plight of the inhabitants of Wonderland is at stake, Alice goes to the wise sage (the caterpillar) and asks for his help. Mr. Caterpillar makes this marvelous statement: "Alice, I can't help you if you don't know who you are."

This book isn't about making you smarter—it's about you finding out who you really are!

Have I caught your eye?
I know you've caught mine
I love the way you smile
You're my perfect design. . .
Don't you know who you are?
You're royalty made to reign with me
Just receive what I've spoken over you
You are the shaper of this generation
Go and release my glory. . .
I've called you shaker the mountains will move where you say.
Now shake the natural and let Heaven reign.

— "You Are" by Josh Ast

CHAPTER ONE

Identity Theft

We were headed home after a two day journey "up north" of our home town of Woodland, Washington, visiting family. A couple hours into our trip and only a mile from our house and those dreaded blue lights began flashing in our rearview mirror. My wife, Lori, was driving and we couldn't have been going more than a few miles an hour over the speed limit. The State Patrolman seemed to be in a pleasant mood and was in a "warning mode" until Lori couldn't find her driver's license. I got out of the car in order to dig through our luggage in the trunk hoping to find the needed identification. I was getting the dreaded feeling of money down the drain as I could not find her wallet and the officer's hand was reaching for pen and ticket book. As he began to record the "pre-ruin the trip home" information, he asked me what my wife's name was. With no trace of Lori's wallet, I turned to him, looked him in the eye and said, "Her name is mud!" A stroke of genius or just plain luck? I don't know! The State Patrolman started laughing, and I figured it was my cue to laugh as well. He put the ticket book away and gave us the "have a nice day and don't forget your license next time" parting comment as he headed back to his car, and we were happily on our way home—no richer, but no poorer! It turned out Lori's wallet was in the trunk after all.

Are you at risk?

Have you ever lost your wallet or purse and had no way to prove your true identity? Try cashing a check without your driver's license. It's not going to happen!

We live in an era when our privacy and "in propria persona" is no longer a luxury to be taken for granted! The legal proof of who you are is at stake along with your ability to function day to day in the normal activities of life.

[handwritten: in the affairs of life. - reign in life]

Identity theft has turned into one of the greatest threats that modern civilization faces.

According to the Office of the Inspector General, "Identity thieves don't steal your money; they steal your name and reputation and use them for their own financial gain. . .Identity theft literally steals who you are, and it can seriously jeopardize your financial future. . .Identity theft is one of the fastest growing crimes in the United States, costing victims over $5 billion annually."

Over 35 million Americans have their personal records exposed to identity theft through business breach annually.

The problems that identity theft cause can inflict pain, confusion, and difficulty on a person, their family and in the work place for years to come, possibly bringing to ruin a person's ability to function in commerce. The residual effect of identity theft is far reaching and strips a person of the influence they were meant to have, potentially making it appear as if the person who was violated no longer exists! There have been at least six million cases of "total" identity theft reported as of 2007, leaving those people virtually powerless to prove who they really are.

> **Rhema Code Truth: If you don't know who you are, no one else will either!**

There is a bigger threat

In the church the problem of, and the consequences of, identity theft is of an even greater concern—not the concern over a person's social security number or checking account, but the crisis of not knowing who we are in Christ and what that means in regard to our life assignment. If our true spiritual identity is stolen from us we will never fulfill our purpose in life.

How big of a deal is it?

In scripture there have been only two groups of people who have had their identity questioned: Adam and Eve when the serpent suggested that who they were was not enough—and Jesus and the many family members subsequent to Him.

There has been an aggressive affront by Satan against God's created family from the beginning as he jealously slandered and dismantled the unique relationship that Father had established with His first Son and Daughter, Adam and Eve. That affront continues today as Lucifer advances his treacherous cause against mankind through every deceitful weapon in his arsenal. In scripture he is called the thief. . .

> *The thief's purpose is to steal and kill and destroy.*
> (John 10:10 NLT)

. . .and he wants to steal your identity, kill you and destroy you! The satanic attack against your life is merciless. Every moment of every day, evil schemes and plots to promote an "identity crisis" in the hearts and minds of believers and unbelievers. He knows the potential that exists in a people who live from the image, nature and likeness of their Creator. When the issue of identity is truly settled within the body of Christ we will become the influencers of nations God intended us to be.

How far does "identity crisis" reach?

Every bias in the history of humanity is rooted in an "identity crisis." Fallen humanity is so locked into evaluating each other from the outside that recorded history is smothered in the atrocities we have placed on each other. From gender bias to racial bias, from economic bias to social bias, from war to war, from genocide to genocide; all rooted in the horrible fear people live in when they try to find their identity from anything apart from who they are "in Christ" on the inside.

To underestimate or miss what has transpired internally through an encounter with Jesus is to give away your world changing influence and to limp through life in a perpetual state of lack—hanging on for a day of hope in the distant future when you meet your Maker and hopefully have your reward in Heaven.

Rhema Code Truth: God's design for your life is one of supernatural influence now!

You were created to impact your environment supernaturally and powerfully as you live from the reality of your true identity as a "son or daughter" of God.

The scope of all God has in store for you is directly connected to you clearly defining your "inner man" identity: the real you, not the one you gaze into the mirror at in the morning, but the one who lives inside of the outer casing called your body. (God gave you a body to assist you in your life's quest of advancing the Kingdom of God. Your body is designed to serve the "real" you, not you serving it.)

You were born to influence the world with the love and goodness of God, but your level of influence will be significantly reduced if you are uncertain of your identity—if you are uncertain of who you really are in Christ!

What has transpired inside of every true believer is stunningly miraculous!

Rhema Code Truth: In Christ, you are offered a literal brand new start—a new birth with a new everything attached to it!

What separates salvation in Jesus from all the other possible pathways to God?

In Christ we are born into a totally new reality with a completely new identity. No other person or deity in the history of mankind has brought such a life altering offer to the table like the one Jesus died and rose again for. You and I are offered a literal brand new start; a new birth with a new everything attached to it. This amazing love offer of God's grace doesn't attach to the old you, it creates a "new" you, releasing you from being defined in any way by the old you. The old you no longer exists thanks to the death Jesus died on our behalf.

> *...you died, and your life is hidden with Christ in God.*
> (Col 3:3)

The intersection of this fabulous life-transforming truth is where the battle line is drawn and conflict rages.

What Jesus has done inside of you is continually being challenged by the satanic influence of this present fallen world.

In the book of Colossians, Paul addresses the need to guard against the onslaught of darkness that is out to corrupt the very thing Christ has accomplished inside of you and me. Paul adamantly exposes the dark strategy that is set on deceiving, cheating, judging and defrauding the Church.

BEWARE:
> *...lest anyone should deceive you with persuasive words...* (Col 2:4)

> *...lest anyone cheat you through philosophy and empty deceit...* (Col 2:8)

> *...let no one judge you...* (Col 2:16)

> *...Let no one defraud you...* (Col 2:18)

The "you" Paul is referring to in these verses is the "you" that's been born into a holy, blameless and irreproachable status in Christ; and these four warnings are signal flares for the body of Christ to block the satanic attack that attempts to neutralize our identity by throwing "religion" and "self-effort" into the mix. If the accuser can get you and I to second guess the great work Jesus has done on our behalf and move us into adding to the process, even subtly, he will effectively take us down a path of ineffectiveness.

Colossians 2 is a magnificent chapter full of the amazing inner transformation that Christ accomplished on our behalf. Paul jealously points us back to the Cross reminding us where we fight from and what we are fighting for:

> *And you, being dead in your trespasses and the uncircumcision of your flesh, He has made alive together with Him, having forgiven you all trespasses, having wiped out the handwriting of requirements that was against us, which was contrary to us. And He has taken it out of the way, having nailed it to the cross.* (Col 2:13-14)

Note here that pre-Christ you were dead, and He alone resolved the problem. He made you alive, for the first time in your existence. He forgave your violation. He erased the written sentence that was against you. He removed it all as He bore it in and on Himself. On the cross He became the ultimate billboard, declaring for all of eternity that what was… is no longer for those who believe!

One of the tactics of darkness is to place the "burden of proof" onto the seen or outer part of our world—to shift our focus onto our outer man and in doing so to thrust us into a "measure up" mentality—one driven by performance and activity. The serpent is still casting a shadow of doubt on God's people attempting to drive them toward a search to truly find themselves. I'm reminded of that line from the movie, *What about Bob*, where Bill Murray whines to Richard Dreyfuss (his therapist), "I need, I need, I need." This is the lie of darkness—that in Christ, we are still in a state of need.

The good news is that "in Christ" we are no longer under the obligation of the law. Our debt is paid in full and we are no longer a needy people. The real you on the inside is totally set free and complete.

> *…if the Son liberates you [makes you free], then you are really and unquestionably free.* (John 8:36 AMP)

Let no one deceive you, cheat you, judge you or defraud you—the price Jesus paid on the cross for you was a great one. It was thorough, lacking in nothing. You were the recipient of the perfect gift, a gift with such power that it shifted you to a whole new reality—you are now hidden with Christ in God. The transformation was so great that you are literally a new person. You are no longer who you used to be!

In Jesus we find our true identity

- Before Jesus. . .there was no you. There was somebody else, but not you.
- He does not add "new" meaning to your life—before Jesus there was no meaning.
- God is not interested in making you a better person. In Christ He has made you a new person.
- Born again is not a fresh start for the same person—it's a new start.
- In Christ you are not an improved version of the old you. You are a brand new you!

What this means is that those who become Christians become new persons. They are not the same anymore, for the old life is gone. A new life has begun! (2 Cor 5:17 NLT)

With these thoughts in mind, I have one question to ask you:

Do you know who you are?

We live in a culture driven and defined by *appearance* and *performance*. People will go to great lengths and spend a fortune on their outward appearance. One young lady who makes her living as an impersonator spent $220,000 to keep her looks current with Britney Spears!

Performance enhancing drugs are turning the world of sports upside down. There is an asterisk next to nearly every modern day sports record. No one is sure what is authentic these days. If someone does exceptionally well the suspicion of "being juiced" hangs over them. People all around the world are struggling to find themselves, to find some form of self expression that will bring definition to their lives.

Is the church any different? My experience tells me no! Though many people carry the title "Christian" they are swallowed up by the world's standard of "finding themselves" or they fall prey to a "religious system" that chews them up and spits them out—never giving them the chance to live "from" the inheritance God has procured for them.

In the Christian world the introspection level is so high that people are paralyzed with suspicion of their own depravity; "guilty until proven innocent," which is often nurtured by their leaders and their own sense of duty to perform and measure up. Or, on the other side of the coin, the substance of people's belief system is so trivial that there is no noticeable distinction that would identify them with anything that resembles a true follower of Christ!

In Brenning Manning's book, *The Furious Longing of God,* he makes this great statement: "I've decided that if I had my life to live over again, I would not only climb more mountains, swim more rivers, and watch more sunsets; I wouldn't only jettison my hot water bottle, raincoat, umbrella, parachute and raft; I would not only go barefoot earlier in the spring and stay out later in the fall; but I would devote not one more minute to monitoring my spiritual growth, no not one!"

In general there are two responses from people who find themselves in performance-driven "churchianity" *(get on God's good side, live a righteous life, stop sinning, obey the rules and pursue a holy lifestyle—that is in fact undoable):*

- One is to work harder!
- One is to give up!

You'll find many people in both camps; some working hard to become something they can't contribute to by their own effort to become and others giving up on the idea realizing the impossibility of the quest. Both create a sense of disillusionment and often cynicism.

I look back over the years with names and faces coming to mind left and right; people who had life-altering encounters with Jesus yet never had a grasp on their transformed identity, forever living from an old mindset, an old identity and an old nature. They were never able to overcome life-plaguing issues and ended up shipwrecked. These were people who could have lived amazing power-filled lives had they embraced the full scope of what God had done inside of them—*a complete transformation into a new reality*, no longer viewing life and self from what was and no longer having to fight the issues that harassed them that in reality no longer existed!

My heart hurts when I think of one of our neighbors years ago—a good guy with a great family but mired in the ongoing struggle he had with his pre-Christ life. He was never able to overcome the lingering thought of who he used to be, never able to break free from that "old man," or experience any kind of lasting victory that comes from embracing a new identity in the present tense. He was forever plagued with the impossible task of trying to measure up to a standard of who he was hoping to become someday. Frustrated in his fight to become righteous and victorious, my friend soon stopped fighting and walked away from God. He gave in to something that no longer existed except in his mind. It breaks my heart to watch people place more power in a lie than in the truth and miss out on such an outrageous experience of living as a "Son or Daughter" of God.

Lori and I have been Senior Leaders of a church called The Promise for 22 years. One of the core values we nurture within The Promise culture is that the reality of God is designed to hit you right in the heart and destroy your old reality and bring you fully into His—pulling you from darkness into light, from sadness to gladness into His presence and into His glory.

Living in His world is when you and I have an encounter that turns into an ongoing reality that transforms our lives so radically that we begin to understand exactly who He is and who we are in Him and what that means.

> **Rhema Code Truth: Authentic inner transformation is not a theory, it's not a hope, it's not a teaching**—it's a world changing reality.

Identity Shift

The Rhema Code identity shift is not a theory; it's not a hope; it's not a teaching. . .it's a reality.

It's the product of an authentic encounter with Miraculous God.

The result: you are not only saved, but radically transformed into a completely different person; no longer limited by the lack of this reality but living from the inexhaustible resources of Heaven—a person with a whole new bloodline and identity, one that springs forth from the magnificent reality of who God is and who we are in Him!

Embracing the full ramifications of our completely new identity in Christ is the first and foremost step in becoming a powerful contributor in the advancement of God's Kingdom on earth. We will never effectively make God "big" if we don't embrace ourselves as "big" in Him.

As you begin to walk in this amazing *rhemalation*, let no one take it from you. You, in fact, are supernatural, amazing and miraculous; and you are a living revelation of God to this world.

Go ahead! Go for it! Take the invitation that God is offering you. It's an invitation into His world, the Kingdom. That's right, that's the good news of the Gospel—God's invitation to you and me is an invitation into a reality far superior to the one we see every day through our natural eye. Jesus is God's love gift to you and me, and He is pulling you into His world if you let Him.

How do you let Him? Change the way you think. Change where you think from! With a new identity comes a whole new thinking process.

A true revelation of Jesus "in you" includes a revelation of you in you. That's right. It starts with how you think about the new you on the inside and then how and where you think from and who you think with (we'll get to that later).

It is truly a new mindset, or as Paul writes in Col 3:1-2, a new place to set your mind:

> *If then you were raised with Christ, seek those things which are above, where Christ is, sitting at the right hand of God. "Set your mind" on things above, not on things on the earth.*

Setting your mind on things above is "thinking" from His world; you have been transformed into an amazing reality that will only have full effect on your life if you come into alignment with your thinking and His.

> *...you, who once were alienated and enemies in your mind by wicked works, yet now He has reconciled in the body of His flesh through death, to present you holy, and blameless, and above reproach in His sight.*
> (Col 1:21-22)

Recieved • (done) Now Walk

You no longer are who you were. That old you is so dead it is as though he or she never existed. What a deal, you are now blameless, holy and above reproach! You are His offspring, born of incorruptible seed by the grace of God. With this in mind Paul writes these next words in Col 2:6-7:

> As you therefore have received Christ Jesus the Lord, so walk in Him, rooted and built up in Him and established in the faith, as you have been taught, abounding in it with thanksgiving.

We are encouraged and admonished to embrace the full scope of our new identity in Jesus and live from it.

I am complete in Him

The fabulous reality of the complete work of Christ "in you" leaves no room for a mediocre assessment of your personal identity. You are not a flawed work in progress battling against your sinful tendencies:

completed work of Christ in me

> For by grace you have been saved through faith, and that not of yourselves; it is the gift of God, not of works, lest anyone should boast. For we are His workmanship, created in Christ Jesus for good works, which God prepared beforehand that we should walk in them. (Eph 2:8-10)

That's right. We are His workmanship and Jesus did all the work. Now, we get "to be!"

Hey! It's time to stop looking back—no more living from what was and no more living toward what will be! It's our time to live from what is. Jesus has saved us from what was and set us on a course to partner with Him to change the world. Come on…step up to the plate, you are amazing and you are a world changer because of what He has done and because He says so!

give place to what is; to this

Your flame burns in every part of me, I want nothing more
Than your flame moving all around me, I've got to have you Lord
Your love it's what set me free, I want nothing more
Your love it's got a hold of me, and you never let go
I want to burn for you, I want to see the world see
To burn in you, be the light of the world

— "Burn" by Casey Schang

CHAPTER TWO

No Matter How it Tastes, Sounds, Feels, Smells or Looks!

Our identity in Christ is such a colossal topic! Embracing the full impact of the amazing and dramatic shift that Jesus works in us at conversion is not only the core of all we are, it impacts everything we believe, say and do. Once you get "it," nothing is left untouched by it! Every part of personal life and ministry is directly influenced by the revelation of who we are in Christ and by the miraculous way God gifts us with the title of "son or daughter."

Five years ago, after being Senior Leaders of The Promise for nearly 15 years and involved in pastoral ministry for over 20 years, Lori and I were about to find out how big of a deal an "identity shift" really was. Instead of teaching about Him and reminding people what they were supposed to be doing for Him, we were heading for a head-on collision with God that was about to change our message forever. All the "do" stuff and all of the "information" was about to take a back seat to the revelation of a radical identity transformation that takes place when a human being encounters Father's love through Jesus.

> *Jesus said. . . "I am the way, the truth, and the life. No one comes to the Father except through Me. If you had known Me, you would have known My Father also. . ."* (John 14:6-7)

Jesus is the access point of our "identity shift." Through Him we meet the Father and become sons and daughters.

The following is a brief sketch of the journey God took us on to help us really "find ourselves" *in Him*.

"Scott! How desperate are you for Me? How bad do you want Me to be 'authentic' in your church world?"

You see, this question that God dropped in my lap one morning several years ago was the leading question of God's response to a heart cry for more of Him and a paradigm shift we had been making for some time. I suppose it started with me and Lori primarily, but in hindsight it was a work of the Spirit in progress in the hearts of many of our church family.

We had come to a crossroad in our style and content of church life as leaders, and it wasn't working out that well for us. Nothing blatantly wrong, no errors in doctrine; we weren't burned out. But there was just nothing that we wanted to keep doing the way we had been. It was like looking at a picture and knowing something was amiss but not quite able to identify what it was. Personally, I had had enough! I knew it, and I think God was just waiting for me to come to that conclusion. It was time to stop "doing church" and time to start "being the church."

For years one of our slogans has been, "We don't go to church, we are the church," but I'm not sure we really had that phrase figured out in its fullest yet.

Don't take me wrong. We had a great local church in a brand new building on 20 beautiful acres right in the middle of our growing community. We had great people and we had great services with great music and great children's ministry and a thriving youth ministry. We had great leaders trained and actively functioning, and we had the presence of God in our meetings… and no one ever got offended and left the church. Okay…except for that last part, the rest is all accurate! But somehow "our" big picture just wasn't what it was supposed to be. We worked hard at ministry and seemed to be so close to the target yet never quite there—wherever "there" was.

It seemed like we were in a perpetual mode of recycling people. We were increasing in numbers, but the content was in question and the revolving door syndrome was, let's just say, unattractive. The model that I had followed and been trained under and attempted to duplicate had lost its luster. I felt like we were giving away a message of hope that was directing people toward some elusive goal they were supposed to shoot for but the target was ambiguous at best and not really achievable. We were solid on the fundamentals: live lives that are God honoring, resist sin, love your neighbor, work hard to measure up, be committed, pay your tithes, put God first, love the lost, give to the mission field, obey, trust, go to church, forgive and the list goes on.

Everything pointed people in the right direction but left them in an unhealthy "pursuit" mode. We were promoting a performance-based approach to God, while not even meaning to; it all sounded right and true but it was putting the "cart in front of the horse."

> **Rhema Code Truth: In our walk with God we cannot afford to put "doing" in front of "being."**

In the midst of our journey this nagging question kept rising up: what results were our church activities really producing? I had come to the point that if I heard one more leader at a conference ask "How many people are you running now," I would run the risk of screaming, and I don't do that kind of thing.

I think there was a bit of unrest in both parties—mine and God's. On my side it was the nagging thought of *"What are we actually doing?"* Are we really impacting anything significantly or at least to the degree or measure that God seems to suggest we should? On God's side it seemed He was suggesting that maybe we should take a few steps back and really evaluate if we were actually incorporating Him into the process or just a portion of Him that seemed to fit our agenda and comfort level.

His next question had me looking out of the side of my eye (that's gunslinger lingo for watching for any possible ambush). As I pondered the ramifications, He questioned, "Do you want more of Me and my presence no matter how it looks, sounds, feels, tastes or smells? And if you say 'yes,' will you really mean it?" What great questions! He had just pulled the carpet out from under any possible personal agenda. [As a side note: when we said yes to His offer I had no idea what I was getting into. I had no context for the degree of change I was about to experience and witness. We were about to go through the most exhilarating, challenging and potentially offensive and misunderstood season of all of our lives combined.]

We had been asking God to take us on an authentic journey that would allow us to experience His presence in ways we had only heard of or read about. We wanted a manifestation of His presence that burned in hearts and moved people to want to press into Him more and more. He was about to give us what we were asking for, if we gave Him what He was asking for.

I could almost hear the still small voice of the Holy Spirit saying, "Do you trust me?"

I have learned over the years and am still learning that when God asks something of us, it will be naturally impossible; and what He really wants is for us to lean into Him and yield to what He wants to do through us.

By this point in my life the possible people-related fallout from saying a resounding "yes" to God held much less influence over me than what it would look like if I politely declined God's open door.

I wasn't born yesterday. I knew what God was inferring. It was not only possible but obvious that what He had in mind was a bit different than what I had in mind when it comes to a significant manifestation of God's presence. Answering this question in the affirmative wasn't going to necessarily put me at the top of the list in a popularity contest.

It's experiences like these that God recommends a thorough mental recording of the moment for future reference and reminder. When the external temptation and pressure to digress becomes great, we have to be thoroughly rehearsed in our core values.

Anytime a fresh move of God arises it will be subject to the scrutiny of many lenses and many voices will arise from the midst of the onlookers. Not all of them will be friendly and supportive.

> **Rhema Code Truth: Our love for Jesus must have a tighter grip on our hearts than the voices and faces around us!**

Authentic or Comfort Zone?

People are certainly creatures of habit and many times habits get misidentified as God's will. I don't want to be a "creature of habit" who leads people in a certain groove because "we've always done it that way." At this point in my life it was time to move forward—even if it meant going where no man had gone before. It was time to break the power of compromising comfort zones.

God was incorporating a new paradigm for us to live from and we had no pattern to follow.

The Shift

Over the weeks and months ahead, the Holy Spirit would ask me certain questions whenever I faced a "sacred cow" of my own or the church family did. The question would go something like this: "Who told you it was supposed to look that way?" or "Why do you do that?"

In other words, there were different ways for things to look and different approaches to take than what the church had been taking through years of. . ."This is how we have always done it and this is how we will keep doing it." Each time we came to a bump, I would pass along the question of the Holy Spirit's to our people as we began to embrace a new way of thinking in our approach to church life: "Who told you it was supposed to look that way?"

"The Holy Spirit would regularly challenge us with this question when it came to our corporate gatherings, "who told you it was supposed to look like that?"

My church family was slowly making a shift from a "gathering" culture to an "empowering" culture—from concern over numbers, names and noses to what the real life fingerprint of God was producing "to, in, and through" His sons and daughters. It was a shift from subtle legalism to a culture of grace, freedom and honor; from seeking God from a distance to living in intimacy. I witnessed the church changing to a core value of wanting His presence more than a concern for people's religious comfort level and to a culture of honor, trust and belief in people rather than a suspicion of their depravity, which often leads to a controlling leadership philosophy enforced by rules and regulations.

We were learning who we are in Him and we were giving God room to move no matter how it looked, sounded, tasted, felt or smelled. We had just released the reins to the Master with a resounding "yes" at all costs, "We want you God and we want our walk with you to be authentic!"

What an explosion began to take place! He wasn't kidding! If we would let Him do it His way, He would show up. Things began to happen. In services His presence would just "be" there and our worship would go on for hours. At times from 10 a.m. to 1 or 2 in the afternoon we would worship—and worship was taking on a whole new look. We were coming into a whole new appreciation for "decent and in order." God was sweeping us off our feet; taking us to a new place of intimacy in Him. It was both wonderful and wild at the same time.

It was an amazing new reality we were all experiencing. We had entered a new prophetic level in God with many elements to it that were new to most of us. We were experiencing supernatural manifestations day and night, and people did not want to leave our meetings. Our young people were absolutely engaging God and we could hardly get them to go home. On one Sunday morning I asked the whole church family who would like to live on The Promise Campus and two-thirds of them raised their hand with a resounding cheer. We were experiencing the birth of a new reality—interestingly, it was one we previously thought we were already a part of.

One Reality...Two Reactions

There were those who were being radically encountered by the Holy Spirit and there were those who were mortified by what they saw and heard—and everything in between those two points was happening all at the same time.

It was fascinating to watch the varying responses: to observe people's reactions based on their different backgrounds relating to God's presentation of Himself; to watch some walk out of our meetings in anger as the presence of God was so thick and powerful, yet their religious training gave them no grid to recognize Him. How amazing it was to see two people sitting virtually side by side and have such contrasting experiences with God—one absolutely loving it, and one not even recognizing God in the midst.

Along with the increased manifestation of His presence came a shift of revelation in regard to His agenda that required some serious adjustment on the part of the church family. From the style of music to the personalization of the Gospel, adjustments were being required on all fronts. God was challenging and confronting attitudes, agendas, preconditioned teaching, identity, personal responsibility, capacity to love, motives. You name it, He was bringing it all to the surface to see if it would pass the litmus test of His heart of love and His will.

It is truly one thing to want all of God and to see His power—and it is a good thing. It's another thing to embrace it and let it happen. I'm not sure if people, especially leaders, know how many things they need to disconnect from their preconceptions and assumptions to allow God to be and do what He wants to be and do in their lives.

Consider pastors. They have budgets, bills and "success" to be concerned about. If God shows up and things get messy or a little out of the ordinary and people get a little nervous, or a lot nervous, and tithes slack off as they use it to make a statement, or just up and leave and go to a different "family;" well, you can see what I am saying. The pastor's reputation is at stake, the drive for numbers to measure success may be at stake, or the esteem in the eyes of people and their peers may be at stake. There is a lot at stake here! I mean, even Jesus had to lean into God and say, "Not my will but yours be done."

Temporary, personal comfort and the will of God don't always go hand in hand. God has a much bigger game plan than most of us do. He wants to impact the world with the Good News of His Kingdom and spread His elaborate love all over the human race, and He's looking for people who are fed up with the status quo and are willing to lay it all out on the line, fearlessly stating, "God, I want you more than anyone or anything."

As God began to breathe on all of us and miracles and healing began to take place on a regular basis, I would share enthusiastically what was happening with my peers. I can't count the times I was asked how it was affecting our "numbers and finances." The question was beginning to bother me until the Lord reminded me that I used to ask similar questions or at least think similar thoughts.

As a leader here is what I have had to pray over and again: "God, all of my worn out preconceptions and sacred cows I throw onto the same dung heap that the Apostle Paul was confronted with. If it's not You and Your way, I don't want it! If people don't understand or whatever, it's okay. I love them and believe your best for their lives." I choose to live as Jesus lived—making the Father's will my personal priority. We only have one opportunity to do this thing right while on earth. After that we will never be able to do in Heaven what we are assigned to do here on earth.

As leaders, if we find our identity in how many people we have in our church or how many we are "getting" to come to our church services, we will be more concerned with the voice and opinion of people than God's! Do we really want radical life-transforming increase—increase that impacts the culture around us and not just what happens inside our buildings? Then we can't be afraid of having people misinterpret what they see when God shows up.

> **Rhema Code Truth: The fear of losing people can't override the passion to empower people.**

The fear of losing people can't override our passion to empower people and our passion for His manifest presence.

In the book of Acts 2:12 there were three responses to the amazing outpouring of the Holy Spirit which preceded a phenomenal harvest of souls into the Kingdom—*some people were amazed, some were perplexed, and others mocked!*

These types of reactions can't be allowed to influence our decisions. Can you imagine what would have happened following Pentecost if Peter would have been intimidated into being more aware of the popular opinions around Him than what was now within him? What if he had listened to the voices of those who had not had an encounter with the Holy Spirit? Can you imagine what church life would look like today? Well, maybe you can. We will face all kinds of reactions from all kinds of people when God shows up, so we have to establish our priorities. Do we want God or do we want man's approval?

It would be so awesome if everyone was "amazed" when they walk into our culture at The Promise and often many are, including me, but we have our share of those who are perplexed and a handful of those who mock. It's okay. It really is. We make room for that. It is not a part of God's agenda to make everybody comfortable with Himself, nor does He try to make people uncomfortable on purpose. It is the reality of Heaven splashing on us and around us when He shows up. It's a definite clash of worlds and we like His better.

Trying to adapt the presence and power of God to fit into this fallen reality is unrealistic and actually ineffective and quite boring. He is inviting us into His world which looks, tastes, sounds, feels and smells quite a bit different from the one we have carved out here.

Have you ever thought about the "...on earth as it is in Heaven" part of the prayer in Matt 6:10? Really, do we even consider what we are praying when we pray that prayer? That is really a radical prayer! If we have a preconceived agenda of how that is supposed to look, we are going to narrow down the possibilities considerably. This is much more than a token prayer. This is a life assignment. If we are going to be a part of releasing Heaven on earth we better have a handle on what really moves us—God or people's opinions / circumstances.

Jesus was planning ahead when He asked Peter by the lake if he loved Him more than all of these in John 21:15. Three times Peter is hit with the same line of questioning. It was as if Jesus was making a deep impression on Peter. "If you are going to effectively empower people Peter, you will have to have an immovable core value of loving Me. Otherwise their pull on your heart and mind will be too strong. Instead of you bringing them up, they will bring you down!"

Here's the story: A handful of Jesus' followers were wandering around with nothing significant to do now that Jesus was gone so they decided to go fishing with Peter. Following a "fishless" night they spotted Jesus on the shore (appearing for the third time since His resurrection) and He directs their attention to the other side of the boat that ends up in a net-filling catch for these tired fishermen. Following this supernatural moment, they work their way to shore to join Jesus for some breakfast:

> *So when they had eaten breakfast, Jesus said to Simon Peter, "Simon, son of Jonah, do you love Me more than these?"*
> *He said to Him, "Yes, Lord; You know that I love You."*
> *He said to him, "Feed My lambs."*
> *He said to him again a second time, "Simon, son of Jonah, do you love Me?"*
> *He said to Him, "Yes, Lord; You know that I love You."*
> *He said to him, "Tend My sheep."*
> *He said to him the third time, "Simon, son of Jonah, do you love Me?" Peter was grieved because He said to him the third time, "Do you love Me?"*
> *And he said to Him, "Lord, You know all things; You know that I love You."*
> *Jesus said to him, "Feed My sheep."* (John 21:15-17)

At this point of the conversation if I'm Peter, I'm starting to think maybe Jesus is trying to tell me something. This could be a "core value" that Jesus is expressing here—a value that all other values are built upon.

Jesus offers no explanation for this discourse. It's a thread in the tapestry of Peter's journey woven to serve him at a later time. It's Jesus cementing into Peter a core value of intimacy that would launch him into being a fearless world changer, empowered by the Spirit and on task to carry the mantle of Revivalist at all cost—uncompromising and undeterred by the winds of adversity and the voice of the unbelieving.

Intimacy is that place of uncompromising love relationship with God. It's the condition of two hearts so inseparable that the integrity of the relationship is never threatened. No outside force or voice of influence has a chance at derailing the kind of intimacy that Jesus offers us. It's a love worth dying for. It's the picture of a son or daughter in a parent's arms, totally secure in who he or she is. It's this kind of intimacy that suffocates fear and intimidation and releases sons and daughters to stand up strong when the odds seem stacked against them. It's the core-value that all other values are built on!

Rhema Code Truth: Intimacy is the birthing of our identity in Christ.

The Pressure to Conform

The pressure to conform to the voice of "reason" is intense for leaders.

Thank God Peter remembered his "hands on moment" with Jesus by the fire that morning. He didn't allow the mockers or those who couldn't figure it out or those who had never done it like that before to influence the move of God.

I love these next words from Acts 2:14:

> "But Peter, standing up with the eleven, **raised his voice**. . ."

No intimidation, no concern for the perceived awkwardness of the "Pentecost" moment, just plain old bold passion and Holy Spirit anointing launching a world shifting message!

I wonder how many times Peter thought back to that moment on the lake shore with Jesus; that morning when he was exasperated with Jesus' line of questioning?

One thing I know. When God shows up "His" way, we better have this core value working in us if we want to stay the course and see the reality of God invading this world through an authentic expression of Kingdom believers!

I am far more interested in what moves God's heart than I am in what moves people. My love for Him is of greater value than the voices of those afraid of doing things out of the norm. This core value has served me well. I hope it will for you also.

One thing leads to another

Being led into this marvelous place of intimacy was the precursor into a life-altering revelation of our identity in Christ. Not only was God "really" showing up, He was showing us some pretty amazing stuff about Himself and about us. It was a whole new world He was leading us into—the world of His Kingdom. Papa (as we are fond of calling Him) was opening our eyes to a whole new way of viewing Him; a new way of viewing ourselves, a new way of talking about Him, a new way of talking about ourselves and a new way of expressing our love for Him, including in the lyrics of our songs.

A prophetic mantle was released on our worship team and a flurry of powerful songs with a distinct Kingdom message began to surface in volumes. We had to rewrite many of the lyrics of songs we had previously used in worship and stop using some totally. There was certainly a pointed culture shift taking place. It became imperative that the church family come into agreement with God's heart on all issues including adjusting our conversation about Him and ourselves. We could tell when we were in danger of grieving the Spirit in worship when we were singing lyrics that were contrary to His nature and His marvelous work of grace in our hearts.

God was leading us into a whole new perspective in relating to Him in worship. Instead of being fearful of taking any of the glory away from Him. we were learning to celebrate our status as sons and daughters as a key element in giving Him glory. No longer leaning into a "woe is me; sad sinners on the road to recovery" type of lyrics, we were learning to agree with His greater reality and our role in it. To declare our amazing status in Christ was not only appropriate but necessary in creating the kind of culture that advances His Kingdom.

Amazing is a two-way street

One of the greatest identity hurdles I have watched people face was the truth that God is amazing and therefore so are they. It seemed that it was easier for people to believe that a false sense of humility and self-degradation made it easier to access His heart.

It was almost comical to watch people get over the idea that their personal poverty was and is not pleasing to God. On a regular basis we encouraged people to look at someone in the eye and tell them, "You are amazing." For some it took weeks to make a shift in their minds that God in fact does love them and is not mad at them. For some they could not get past the perception of their own personal post-Jesus depravity. They had been so entrenched in a religious spirit that they were stuck—sometimes even angry at the suggestion that they were in any way "amazing."

We began to realize that the greatest expression of worship we could offer God was an accurate assessment of our status as sons and daughters through what He had done for us. No more futile apologies for our state of depravity and no more stereotypical "Christianese" like "unmerited favor" defining His act of Grace on our behalf. No more fear of falling into some pride thing by announcing our personal amazing position as Royalty in Jesus.

As Lori and I, and our amazing leadership team who never hesitated for one second, have leaned into "No matter how it tastes, sounds, feels, smells or looks," it has been incredible to say the least. I am so proud of our Promise Family who has weathered this paradigm shift.

We are not the same as we were a handful of years ago and we certainly have more to walk into as God continues to pour out His Rhema Code "to us, in us and through us." While we are learning to "yield, be, say, and do" and fall madly in love with Him and each other, we are at the same time having the time of our lives.

*I am in orbit my life revolves around the Son
I am in motion with the Spirit who raised the Son
And also raised me, Jesus you saved me*

....

*I am the light that shines to complement the Son
I am on fire with the Spirit who raised the Son
And also raised me, Jesus you saved me*

....

*We dance we dance to show the world
That He lives He lives he's living through us
We dance we dance freed by His power
We live we live a living miracle*

....

*I was made to live beyond what I can see
I am called to defy this reality*

Its my own personal reality

— "Live Through Me" by Casey Schang, Robbie Wilbur, Josh Ast

CHAPTER THREE

The Next Great Move of God... You!

A fresh outpouring of revelation and calling is upon us—and you, the individual, who make up the church and are the target of this outpouring. The trumpeter has released the sound of the trumpet and the hosts of Heaven are at attention for this great move of God. If you listen closely you can hear it—the voice of God calling you to your destiny. It's what you were made for. It's what makes sense of all this crazy stuff going on all around us. You and I have a role to play; as a matter of fact, we are the key players in this unfolding story of human history. We are not an afterthought, waiting for some distant hope, some far off day when all will be well with our soul! We are living in a very present, real time, right now—Christ in you; you are the light of the world—moment!

God is calling you to "be" powerful. His grand design has always had you as the centerpiece of His intention. There is a world out there waiting for the "real you" to show up—the one He has empowered to bring resolve and solution to the predicament of a fallen race of people. The message is the "Kingdom," and you are the messenger!

The voice of change in the morning

It was an early morning weekday about eight years ago while I was in my office minding my own business that God solidified a shift in my approach to Church Leadership and people development—a shift that would literally change the course of our lives and the lives of those Lori and I were leading. He began to ask me a series of questions that were "set up" questions—the kind that you know better than attempt to answer; the kind that He's not really looking for an answer for His sake!

The first question went something like this: "Scott, as a Leader what kind of people are you hoping to end up with?" My response was along this line, "Um, I'm not sure." He went on, "As you lead this church, what are you hoping to produce?" Again my answer had the strong sound of "um" and "uh." It was obvious that He was bringing to my attention the glaring gap between my ideas and His desire. In the course of our one-sided dialogue that morning He made it clear that He had a much higher goal for His church than I did. I had been on a quest to help people get some relief from their sin predicament via salvation and hopefully some self-improvement, i.e. some character development, relationship help and so forth, while He was thinking on a much grander scale—a much bigger picture!

"Scott! I want you to raise up World Changers—a new species of people, a supernatural generation of believers; those that will accurately reflect me on this planet. I want you to raise up fearless people who really know who their Father is and what it means to have Me living inside of them, a people who will not only give me glory but bear My Glory as I reveal myself *to them, in them and through them.*"

It was the continuation of a paradigm shift that the Holy Spirit had been revealing to Lori and me over the previous few years; but this step in the shift left no room for foggy uncertainty. He is on the move and is pouring out a now word—a Rhema Word—that is world shaking and church shaking, both at the same time!

Like a million laser pointers shining on one target, God had just clarified our assignment: "You are now going to spend yourself on bringing to people's attention who they really are in Me and what it means to live from their new identity."

No longer would we be limiting our ministry approach to a rescue mindset that based its energy on "gathering" people and gauged success on how many attended meetings, but on an "empowering" agenda that lovingly challenged people to rise to the occasion of how amazing God is and what that means to those who choose to host Him internally. We would be ministering to those who would get the full impact of what it means to be born again.

Being born again, again

In the months and years that have followed that early morning chalk talk, I have witnessed time and time again one of the most rewarding things I have ever experienced pastorally. It is the "born again, again" phenomena; the radical life-altering, post-salvation experience of a believer's awakening to the magnitude of just what Jesus accomplished at Calvary on their behalf. The powerful force of those amazing words Jesus spoke before He died on that cross: "It is finished." Those words launch you and me far "beyond salvation" into an unseen reality far superior to any seen or natural thing. That "born again" is far more than a fresh start and a slate wiped clean, but a literal "Identity shift" complete with a new spiritual DNA from Heaven.

Who's your Daddy?

"Our Father" is more than an opening line in a prayer: it is the foundation of our identity. It's the beginning phrase on our birth certificate. It's what validates our position as sons and daughters.

Lori and I are grandparents now. Though it is a bit surreal still, I am getting used to being addressed as "Papa" by first born grandson Laik, who because of the hold he has on my heart, now has ownership of up to half of my kingdom, which technically doesn't exist because I have "given" it away so many times that I'm sure it's been reduced to a sixteenth by now.

There is nothing on this planet that could ever challenge Laik's position as our grandson and son of our son, Casey, and our wonderful daughter-in-law Ashley. At conception it was forever decided by virtue of his DNA, who Laik is! There was no price Laik had to pay to be who he is; the family line was a done deal for him.

As good as it is having one grandson, along comes Rais, grandson number two, and my kingdom has shrunk again. Rais's name means chief or leader, and I'm sure his name is prophetic by natural confirmation—that boy can let out a cry! From birth to the time of this writing, at a whopping four months old, when Rais wants something done he is not afraid to let everyone within a one block radius know that there are things that need attending to. What a contrast in scenes—from Rais's goo-goo, sweet dimple-faced smile that captivates all attention to that ear piercing "attention all listeners" heads up that has the ability to gain more attention when it didn't seem like there was any left over from his smile.

I will never be able to separate the scene of Rais developing his leadership gift (that amazing cry) from the Holy Spirit's declaration of our sonship and daughterhood seen in Gal 4:4-7:

> *When the fullness of the time had come, God sent forth His Son, born of a woman, born under the law, to redeem those who were under the law, that we might receive the adoption as sons. And because you are sons, God has sent forth the Spirit of His Son into your hearts, crying out, 'Abba, Father!' Therefore you are no longer a slave but a son, and if a son, then an heir of God through Christ.*

I find it fascinating and so appropriate that the language in these verses describe so accurately the birthing process, including the familiar cry of a new life—a new life birthed in the heart of an individual who yields to the radical DNA life-altering shift from Heaven, confirmed by the Holy Spirit's crying out: "You now have a new Dad and everything has changed and nothing will ever be the same!"

May that cry, blended with your cry, forever seal the deal—if you are in Christ, you are a son or a daughter! You are the King's child and there is no Plan B.

Don't let the word adoption mislead you into thinking this was an afterthought kind of deal. On the contrary, this is and you are "the deal!" This word "adoption" is not used as we would use it with the idea of adopting a child who didn't previously belong to us. This word is the picture of literally becoming a child—an authentic birthing into a new reality. When you are birthed into the Kingdom you are an official heir with an indisputable genealogy. The magnitude of this reality is what we call "being born again, again." When the light clicks on and you "get" the full wonder of what it means to be a totally "new person" in Christ, the realization of a complete disconnect from the past and a "World Changing" future ahead of you is stunning—stunningly good!

We refuse to be bogged down with the dark weightiness of what "was." In Christ we are not about massaging the past trying to make it go away; we are all about what "is" and being primary partners with Him in the advancement of His Kingdom goodness.

Beyond Salvation: "Fish or cut bait"

Brooklyn was on vacation with her family in Southern California and they were enjoying a stroll on a pier at the beach. While admiring the rows of fishermen, Brooklyn noticed that one of them had reeled in a catch. It was a squid. Not being familiar with the local fishing, she exclaimed, "Look what that man caught." Her husband Nate politely informed Brooklyn that the "catch" was the bait and after a good laugh they both moved on to enjoy more scenery.

Can you imagine how it would be if at the end of the day fishermen were satisfied with the bait? Obviously the bait is important, but it is not the goal.

Sometimes in Christianity it seems there is a preoccupation with the starting point of our spiritual journey. As fantastic as it is to be born again through our loving Savior, it's not the "full meal deal;" it's just the beginning.

Salvation is not the end game—it is the launching point for a life filled with Kingdom adventure and activity. We must not stop at the point of our new birth in Jesus, content with getting "the problem of our lost soul" resolved and preoccupied with "getting better." We need to see what salvation turns us into—what the activation of the blood of Jesus actually does for us and to us.

Rhema Code Truth: By virtue of a new bloodline you "are" amazing and powerful.

In Christ, you are of a bloodline that by its very nature launches you into greatness. It declares to you and on your behalf that "You are amazing and you are powerful."

> *Therefore, since we are the offspring of God, we ought not to think that the Divine Nature is like gold or silver or stone, something shaped by art and man's devising.* (Acts 17:29)

> *His divine power has given to us all things that pertain to life and godliness, through the knowledge of Him who called us by glory and virtue, by which have been given to us exceedingly great and precious promises, that through these you may be partakers* (partners) *of the divine nature...* (2 Pet 1:3-4)

In Christ we have a "nature shift"—off with the old and on with the new—and the new is literally "out of this world."

One of our amazing young guys at The Promise works for a construction company primarily employing people from their particular church group. Joshua is constantly calling out their "amazing" status in Christ and they never know what to do with it. Their regular response is, "We're just sinners saved by grace." They have no context in their paradigm to relate to themselves from any condition other than from lack. They have been trained to look at the work of Christ as a fix for an ongoing condition of depravity and fallen nature.

> **Rhema Code Truth: In Christ we no longer live in a condition of depravity and no longer have a fallen nature—erasing "lack" from our vocabulary.**

Though it may sound spiritual, this idea of, *"humble sinners saved by grace,"* is really a position of spiritual death, one that exonerates the holder of any personal responsibility to live "from" and for anything. Instead of influencing anything or anybody with the power of God working through them, the proponents of this mindset rob themselves of a great and wondrous journey of impact and Kingdom advancement. The ongoing promotion of this mindset has created a void of power and influence in a large portion of the body of Christ.

World Changers

How is God going to impact the world? Through you and me! He has no other plan. The revelation of "you" as the next great move of God is a stunning thought! It leaves no room for observation or a viewer friendly approach to church life. When you embrace the reality of what has transpired inside of you at conversion, you "will" come to the conclusion that you were born for this—it's who you are. It puts teeth to your reason for living in a *now* moment and it makes repulsive the mere suggestion that you only live to exist and get by—hoping for a future day! The day and the time is now. God is calling you up. You are the answer to prayer. You are the one who will show up representing your Father in Heaven—on assignment to bring His reality to the needs of this planet, "On earth as it is in Heaven!"

Our Father! What a great thing to be able to declare and not only declare but to have that truth explosively thrust you into an automatic world influencer and world changer role. You were born for greatness! Your job now is to learn to "live from" that reality!

Live from, not toward...

I can think of no topic more paradigm-shifting for a leader and for those who are being led, than the idea of "living from vs. living toward." As leaders, Lori and I are forever compelled to lead people into their greatness—*from* their current condition of greatness! Living "from" is living out of the context of the complete work of Christ in the heart of a believer, rather than working "toward" some unattainable goal of measuring up to God's standard in a performance-driven paradigm. I will refer to this idea more in Chapter Four. Instead of trying to make people great or strive for greatness or strive for anything for that matter or "become" anything, we have found it to be our leadership mandate to help them live "from" the revelation and reality of who and what they "already are" in Christ.

This is no subtle point. It makes all the difference in our approach to Christianity and our corporate and individual call to advance God's Kingdom.

Living Toward...

I have watched people invest years of their lives and massive amounts of mental, emotional and religious energy on a quest to get "to" some place or condition in God. To really consider themselves accepted, forgiven, loved and qualified for Heaven. I've even encouraged people in the quest; "keep going, don't give up, press in, press on." It all seemed right, noble and even spiritual, with scriptural phrases like, "work out your own salvation" and "pursue holiness" as supporting pillars of the cause. It sounded good, but it wasn't producing fruit that matched up to the amazing reality of Christ "in us." It even became apparent that the "working hard to get there" approach was counterproductive in most, if not all, cases.

As the Holy Spirit began to show me that there was a better "way;" that in fact He had already taken care of the deal for us and given us the job of agreeing with Him, I began to see remarkable transformation take place in the hearts and lives of people. Instead of teaching people to "get better, become holy, become righteous," I began encouraging them to live *from* those conditions: holiness is not an activity and righteousness is not activity-based but are in fact both conditions of grace we are to live "from." Instead of teaching people to do all the right Christian disciplines to get to a place of a God-pleasing lifestyle, I began empowering people to "live from" the reality of those conditions that are part of their birthright in Christ.

Birthright

When the eyes of our understanding are clouded by a performance-based approach to relationships (*what we need to do instead of who we are),* the relational fog often leads people to ask the wrong questions in the middle of relational drama. This is often seen in sons and daughters to mother and father relationships.

In the parable of the lost son in Luke 15, the story line has a father with two sons going in opposite directions in life: one squandering his inheritance with loose living and one faithfully working on the family ranch honoring his dad with discipline and loyalty. Both sons come to wrong conclusions about their approach to Dad's heart. They ask the wrong question! The loose living son essentially asks, "Dad, haven't I lost my place in your heart by all the wrong things I've done?" The loyal son asks, "Dad, haven't I earned a place in your heart by all the right things I have done?" They were both wrong. They were their father's sons—period! Both were unable to add or subtract to the condition of sonship by what they did or did not do.

God removes the relational drama by His dramatic expression of love in the birthing process of new believers. We become sons and daughters as we are born of the Spirit…

> *That which is born of the flesh is flesh, and that which is born of the Spirit is spirit.* (John 3:6)

We have new spiritual DNA along with a new nature, new parents, and a new address:

> *. . .God, who is rich in mercy, because of His great love with which He loved us, even when we were dead in trespasses, made us alive together with Christ (by grace you have been saved), and raised us up together, and made us sit together in the heavenly places in Christ Jesus.* (Eph 2:4-6)

That which was no longer is and. . .

> *Therefore, if anyone is in Christ, he is a new creation; old things have passed away; behold, all things have become new.* (2 Cor 5:17)

. . .we are literally a "new species."

I like the way J.B. Phillips puts the idea of new:

> *By His own wish He made His own sons through the Word of truth, that we might be, so to speak, the first specimens of His new creation.* (James 1:18)

We no longer find our identity in external or temporary realities but resource from an eternal condition called "born again."

We are so used to finding love and identity in what we do that it is a high hurdle to jump over to connect relationally with God on the sole basis of who He is and what He has done on our behalf. All that needs to be done has been done. Father has paid an immense price to put on you and me the title of Son or Daughter.

Son/Daughter or servant? Earlier I made the comment that we are not going to demean the concept of grace by defining it as "unmerited favor." The idea of unmerited favor comes from a servant mentality or theology. Servant mentality causes us to think that we don't deserve the love and favor God has gifted us with. Servant mentality thinks that He in fact overlooks our inadequacy and loves us in spite of our flaws and failures as long as we keep up the good work as a good servant of the King; that somehow He sees us through a "blood" covering and is able to look past our depravity.

The good news is that what was unpresentable to God no longer exists, and now as believers we hold the title of Son or Daughter that puts us in the category of an Heir or Heiress. We don't live in undeserved or unmerited favor. That would imply that we are still fallen. Actually the opposite is true. We are very favored by God. He didn't do a half-baked job on us. The only way to give Him full credit is to recognize how He has fully transformed us. When we get past a "servant mentality" and embrace the title Son or Daughter we will truly become effective "servants," finally being able to serve His kingdom purpose because we "get to," from who we "are" instead of "have to," out of duty. Then serving becomes a pleasure and a powerful tool in advancing the Kingdom.

Living "from" is such an amazing honor—no longer working "towards" or in a performance-based approach to God but living "from" our birthright. When we get a hold of this truth watch out… this is when things get very exciting!

Living from the inside out

> *…He would grant you, according to the riches of His glory, to be strengthened with might through His Spirit in the <u>inner man</u>, that Christ may dwell in your hearts through faith; that you, being rooted and grounded in love, may be able to comprehend with all the saints what is the width and length and depth and*

height —to know the love of Christ which passes knowledge; that you may be filled with all the fullness of God. Now to Him who is able to do exceedingly abundantly above all that we ask or think, according to the power that works <u>in us</u>... (Eph 3:16-20)

Rhema Code Truth: Living in a "from" paradigm is an "inside" job.

Lori's gift: some people just have a knack for looking good in certain things. My wife is one of those people. She looks good in anything for that matter, but in this case she just makes any coat look great. Whenever we are out shopping (yes, I love to shop! Don't all men?). . . Anyway…whenever we are out shopping we seem to find ourselves in the women's department checking out the latest fashion in women's coats. It's actually a bit unusual. We can find a coat on the rack that looks just okay, but as soon as Lori puts the coat on it seems to transform into an excellent article of clothing. I mean as soon as she is inside of any given coat, the coat seems to take on a new life. In the case of coats, what we have noticed is that Lori defines the coat instead of the coat defining her! This has been a costly reality for us at times but I haven't minded at all.

The point is what's on the inside is obviously the primary focus. We are not defined by what's on the outside, only by what Jesus has done on the inside! The outside is just our "coat" serving the greater cause; the "real us" which is on the inside!

Rhema Code Truth: Living "from" the inside out is priority for successful Kingdom advancement.

One of the things we teach people at The Promise is to learn to resource from the "right" source—that which is eternal vs. that which is temporal. Living from the "inside out" is having what's inside of you influence what's on the outside instead of allowing what's on the outside influence what we call the "real you"—that which is unseen and that which is eternal—the real you on the inside!

In probably the most well known verse in the Bible, John 3:16, God gives us a "heads-up" on a condition that is mandatory to embrace; one that truly defines you and me:

> *For God so loved the world that he gave his only Son, so that everyone who believes in him will not perish but have eternal life.* (NLT)

In Christ we have shifted into a state or condition of "eternal." If you "believe," you shift from temporal to eternal!

Your body is your temporary "coat." It is what the real *"you"* lives inside of—it is no more you than the car you drive or the house you live in or the job you happen to have. Your body is a gift from God, designed to assist you as you live from a *state* of eternity while in a temporary shell.

Rhema Code Truth: In the New Testament era, we are the "Holy of Holies." We are the habitation of God's presence. We no longer have to go through a variety of steps to get to God—we host God!

You are His House!

> *. . .your body is the temple of the Holy Spirit who is in you. . .* (I Cor 6:19)

To look in the mirror in the morning and to read more into that reflection than there really is, is a plague on the body of Christ. We must see past the mirror. We live in a world that evaluates nearly everything from the external and quite often the church expresses this same system of evaluation.

Leaders that grid from the external—who "see" people from the outside—will always look at the natural or outer man they are ministering to and consequently address their people by what they see. God does not do that! He continually addresses the heart of man and pushes us to do the same.

To be or not to be?

In Christ you are not an improved version of what you used to be! You are a brand new you! What once was, no longer is. You have been transformed by His incredible love gift into an amazing, miraculous and perfect creation. This is great news! You and I are no longer defined by anything connected to this world—just His world.

When the Apostle Paul talks about "walking in the Spirit" in Galatians. . .

> *Walk in the Spirit, and you shall not fulfill the lust of the flesh.* (Gal 5:16)

> *. . .If we live in the Spirit, let us also walk in the Spirit.* (Gal 5:25)

. . .he is not addressing some mystical approach of following after God. He is directing our attention to living in and from a condition that transpired at conversion. In Christ, you and I are born of Spirit Seed; we are spirit people, living in and from a Spirit reality. We are no longer of this world though we still live in this world.

In John's Gospel, Jesus is talking about you and me and the transition that took place that enabled us to literally live in two realities at the same time. We live from His reality while on assignment in this reality.

> *...you are not of the world, but I chose you out of the world* (John 15:19)

> *They are not of the world, just as I am not of the world. Sanctify them by Your truth. Your word is truth. As You sent Me into the world, I also have sent them into the world.* (John 17:16-18)

Step away from your skin!

I have used this illustration a variety of times to help people create a visual in regards to the distinction between their body and the "eternal and real" them. As if you could, grab the zipper that holds your body suit on and unzip it. Now step out of and away from your skin. Go ahead, take a look at it. This thing that houses the real you is in fact there to assist you in this journey of advancing God's Kingdom. It is not intended to define you and it will not make it into heaven with you. It is not you! It is your body—the shell that houses you. You are supposed to take care of it; feed it nutritionally, clean it, exercise it and clothe it—but don't by any means let it convince you that "it" is you! I promise it will try to and so will everything around you; every person, every commercial, every teacher, every leader, every mindset and cultural influence. They won't mean to, but they don't know any better. It's so hard for people to separate the two and see the true unseen person inside of the temporal casing they live in. I repeat: that body you live in will go through stuff on a regular basis that will require you to stay on top of your game to identify each accurately (it and you). Don't give it an inch!

As you get older it will try to make you think you are too old for whatever; but the truth is the real you hasn't aged a bit. You never become irrelevant or obsolete. Maybe your body can't do what it used to do but your value never diminishes.

There may be times when you don't "feel" useful or you aren't as accomplished at something as you used to be. The good news is you never grabbed a hold of God's heart by what you could do anyway.

There are three things that are vitally important to hold onto:
- God loves you like crazy!
- The person He loves lives inside of your body and is eternal at the point of new birth.
- The old you no longer exists.

Not long ago I was honored to do the memorial service of a dear friend of mine. As I was preparing for the service the Holy Spirit reminded me of one of the core values He has infused into my ministry grid. It's my anthem: "Whatever You want to say, whatever You want to do, God." I am totally committed to partnering with the Holy Spirit when it comes to communicating His heart publicly. In this case it was going to be among many friends and family of my long-time friend and brother in Christ.

As I was praying and preparing for the right things to say over the course of four or five days before the service, it became clear that God had a bit of an unusual theme for me to share, especially at a memorial service. Apparently the Holy Spirit wanted to deal with some mindsets that were holding people in bondage, plus He was leading me into another season of revelation insight. When He does that I camp there until He says move on and, no matter who He has me speaking to, they get the current stuff.

The message began to unfold like this: I want you to address two groups of people: the first group are those who are unsaved and feeling like they can't come to me because they are unworthy and they think they need to upgrade their lives before they can invite me into their hearts like they've been told they need to do to get to heaven; the second group are those believers who keep trying to make an application of me from a fallen paradigm, those who know that they are supposed to live a lifestyle that reflects their belief system.

Tell both groups that I am not interested in applying my life and my world "onto" theirs. Tell them I'm not interested in them "inviting" ME into their hearts; and furthermore, tell the first group that I realize many of them don't come to me because of people they watch who claim to be Christians but are hypocrites.

Okay Papa. I can do that…I think! This was a memorial service with standing-room only attendance and people who were hurting from the loss of their loved one; but as usual, Papa had a broader stroke of His brush in mind. I knew I didn't have time to develop a teaching, and I hadn't had any previous time to develop any background to the ideas He wanted communicated to these people.

I did what He asked and left the rest up to Him, knowing that He would release prophetic insight into the hearts and minds of those He was drawing out of religious mindsets. Lori and our daughter, Destiny, said it was amazing to watch the Spirit of revelation touch people's hearts. Following the service, the comments from many went as follows: "that was the best memorial service I've been to," "thank you for helping me understand what a hypocrite is," "thank you for such a loving and comforting message."

Although the topic may have seemed a bit odd for the setting, it was as if no one noticed as God's heart was released throughout that gathering. I know I learned a couple of things in that prophetic moment. I learned I can never stray away from my calling to empower people by releasing the revelation of what it means to embrace their true identity in Jesus. The message is applicable in any and every situation.

I know there is a problem with the way Jesus is often presented to the world and the way people are often encouraged to live out their belief system—and what it does to the body of Christ.

Jesus never suggested that He wants people to invite Him into their hearts. In thinking that is the case it potentially leaves a person with the idea that Jesus is going to take them on a long journey of remodeling their lives, when in fact that is far from the case. His goal is actually to kill you (the old you that is) and start over! I know that sounds stunning, but it's good news by the way. Check out the following words from Paul's letter to the Church in Rome:

> *Could it be any clearer? Our old way of life was nailed to the Cross with Christ, a decisive end to that sin-miserable life.* (Rom 6:6 MSG)

It takes away all concern of trying to blend the old with the new and leaves the unbeliever free of trying to resolve his or her past. Remember, God is not interested in giving you a fresh start. He came to give us a brand new start. The Gospel is not a self-improvement program intended to make "you" a better you. His intention is to make you a "new you," to the degree that the old you no longer exists.

> *Therefore, from now on, we regard no one according to the flesh. Even though we have known Christ according to the flesh, yet now we know Him thus no longer. Therefore, if anyone is in Christ, he is a new creation; old things have passed away; behold, all things have become new.* (2 Cor 5:16-17)

The emphasis here is a brand new start and a new perception of where that starting point is; not the exterior or natural part of man, but the eternal and internal man that is not in any way associated or connected to what was. In Christ there is no what was!

The hypocritical people that God directed my attention to for that memorial service are the ones who religiously try to make an application of God's goodness onto an "old" nature mentality. In Christ, man's old nature and His love offer of "new life" do not mix at all and any attempt to apply Jesus to a life that considers itself still fighting against "the old nature" will only result in frustration for the one who attempts to live from their old condition and, unfortunately, for those who observe the process.

> *I have been crucified with Christ; it is no longer I who live, but Christ lives in me; and the life which I now live in the flesh I live by faith in the Son of God, who loved me and gave Himself for me.* (Gal 2:19)

There are two different sets of "I's" being used in this fantastic verse. One is the "before Christ" I and the other is the "in Christ" I. The old "I" no longer exists and the new "I" lives from a whole new reality with a new perception.

Rhema Code Truth: To make any attempt at applying any of the virtues of the Kingdom through a mindset of a fallen grid apart from grace and the complete work of the Cross will only lead to human effort attempting to work out Heavenly 'ideas.'

The danger of applying Jesus to a fallen mindset is equal to attempting to apply the New Covenant to an Old Covenant mindset. The supernatural element required to release the Kingdom through a human life will be bypassed and the fruit of the effort will be limited to natural ability.

Good ideas and good works and good intentions will not advance the Kingdom and will not effectively change spiritual atmospheres. We must embrace "being" supernatural to "do" supernatural things.

Face to Fig Leaf

In scripture, John 8:56-59, Jesus refers to Himself as "I Am."

> *"Your father Abraham rejoiced to see My day, and he saw it and was glad."* Then the Jews said to Him,

> *"You are not yet fifty years old, and have You seen Abraham?" Jesus said to them, "Most assuredly, I say to you, before Abraham was, I AM." Then they took up stones to throw at Him; but Jesus hid Himself and went out of the temple, going through the midst of them, and so passed by.*

Echoing the name for God given to Moses in Ex 3:14:

> *And God said to Moses, "I AM WHO I AM." And He said, "Thus you shall say to the children of Israel, I AM has sent me to you."*

The name I AM is an expression of God's nature. "He is"—not—"He hopes to be "or "He who is shooting to become." I want to propose to you that I AM and "we hope to be" don't blend well. A key component of God's nature is His eternal condition. He is the Alpha and Omega, the Beginning and the End—the Everlasting Father. This aspect of His nature plays heavily in His offer to us of everlasting life.

Somewhere between two million and, let's say, four million days ago, on the sixth day I AM looked at what He had created and said, "It is very good (Gen 1:31)!" I AM only creates very good stuff! Unfortunately not many days later (comparatively speaking) I AM was standing "face to fig leaf" with two people that were now in the category of "you were" and there was the dilemma—the conflict of natures. Mankind had fallen into a condition of incompatibility with their Maker.

Not to worry! God had it all worked out! He was about to break the condition of "you were" off of humanity and restore mankind back to a place of compatibility with Himself. He was on a mission; a mission to re-establish man's lost "eternal condition." This is such good news. Jesus didn't come to make you better, He came to make you new, to give you a new nature, to invite you into I AM's world as a "you are"—not you hope to be, or you are a work in progress.

It is critical to embrace the extent of God's love offer found in John's Gospel, chapter three, verse sixteen. To **believe** in Him is to be thrust into a divine eternal condition that affords compatibility between God and mankind.

Believing is no small thing. It is the core of all things. At the heart of believing is Everlasting Life. Everlasting Life is a complete transformation of natures which includes a complete transformation of realities and core values. Eternal life is not a destination—it's a condition.

Jesus attacks a faulty mindset

In the sixth chapter of John's Gospel, in the midst of a few critical verses is the unusual recap of Jesus' conversation to the crowd who the previous day had been the benefactors of a miracle picnic. They were so impressed by His ability to meet their natural needs that they were inspired to make Him king. This wasn't working into God's game plan so Jesus headed to the other side of the lake. Of course they followed and Jesus in His masterful yet mysterious way continued contradicting every erroneous perception about God's intent and purpose towards mankind.

It's as if He is saying to those listening, "You and I are on very different sides of the coin and to illustrate, I'm about to say a few things that you are totally not going to get as long as you are thinking from this world and as long as you are allowing this fallen reality to speak to you with more influence than you give me."

This is when it gets really good! Jesus is messing with their grid for sure. He uses the miraculous bread moment to illustrate His mission as He lets the bread point to Himself as the true bread of life much to the consternation of the murmuring Jews, "What do you mean you are the bread that came down from heaven?"

> *Most assuredly, I say to you, he who believes in Me has everlasting life. I am the bread of life. Your fathers ate the manna in the wilderness, and are dead. This is the bread which comes down from heaven that one may eat of it and not die. I am the living bread which came down from heaven. If anyone eats of this bread, he will live forever; and the bread that I shall give is My flesh, which I shall give for the life of the world."* (John 6:47-51)

> *The Jews therefore quarreled among themselves, saying, "How can this Man give us His flesh to eat?" Then Jesus said to them, "Most assuredly, I say to you, unless you eat the flesh of the Son of Man and drink His blood, you have no life in you. Whoever eats My flesh and drinks My blood has eternal life, and I will raise him up at the last day. For My flesh is food indeed, and My blood is drink indeed. He who eats My flesh and drinks My blood abides in Me, and I in him. As the living Father sent Me, and I live because of the Father, so he who feeds on Me will live because of Me. This is the bread which came down from heaven — not as your fathers ate the manna, and are dead. He who eats this bread will live forever."* (John 6:52-58)

What a powerful set of verses! Jesus has no interest in drawing a crowd or self promotion in any natural sense. He had one agenda—contradicting a fallen realm that had in its clutches His precious creation. He doesn't bother to qualify His statements because He wasn't doing a teaching. He was making a statement! He was shaking the foundation of unbelief that was smothering mankind. An unbelief that had people glued to the limitations of their natural plight.

Look at the emphasis Jesus makes in declaring His core value to those in attendance. It's a "they said, He said" moment. Following His miraculous arrival on the other side of the lake…

> . . .*they said to Him, "Rabbi, when did You come here?"* (John 6:25)
>
> *Jesus said, "Most assuredly, I say to you, you seek Me, not because you saw the signs, but because you ate of the loaves and were filled. Do not labor for the food which perishes, but for the food which endures to everlasting life, which the Son of Man will give you. . ."* (John 6:26-27)
>
> *Then they said to Him, "What shall we do, that we may work the works of God?"* (John 6:28)
>
> *Jesus …said to them, "This is the work of God, that you believe in Him whom He sent."* (John 6:29)
>
> *Then they said to Him, "Lord, give us this bread always."* (John 6:34)
>
> *And Jesus said to them, "I am the bread of life. He who comes to Me shall never hunger, and he who believes in Me shall never thirst."* (John 6:35)

Each response Jesus gave them, although keying on two separate words, "believe and eternity," was from one context—the context of "His world" and how He was about to restore access into it. Time and time again Jesus draws their attention to a higher place. Even though they kept resourcing from a fallen mindset, yet Jesus was undaunted in delivering a message that is far superior to anything their natural mind could come up with. His was an offer to trade in the limited and temporary for the unlimited and timeless.

The brightest minds in the world will never get His message through informational analysis. It is a message of transformation, not information.

Those in attendance that day were struggling with their "to do" list and Jesus was hitting them where it hurts—flesh, blood and eating—smack dab right in the middle of their rituals.

There was only one way back to "I AM" and it had nothing to do with "do" and everything to do with "believe." I AM was telling them that "I AM" is all you need in order to be "You Are!"

The day of trying to get to God was over. He had come to them but He needed them to get the old system out of their minds. In order to become supernatural any self-effort had to be eliminated. In order to embrace Eternal all temporal had to go.

Can you hear it? God's heart being expressed through Christ: "Believe…believe…believe" or "Engage…engage…engage" or "Think from my world…think from my world…think from my world."

This is the core of "believe"—how you think and where you think from. If you're going to be in His world you have to think "from" it. You have to believe.

Thinking from His world

Believing is one of those words or ideas that are so big it almost hurts to put it into practice. I mean, when you hear the mandate, "You must believe," what does that mean?

We help define "believing" as "thinking from His world." This is one of those truths that make life easier; easier in the sense of making sense of such a monumental core value.

We have all heard many great teachings on "believe," and we are all grateful. But still, if you took a survey and asked people to define what it means to believe you would find as I have that that is a question that is quite difficult for people to answer in any definitive way. You will hear the stock or pat answers and be able to readily identify them: "to trust in, to rely upon, to have faith in," and so on. They are true but just generic enough that the definitions leave little to put your mind into and turn into any appreciable life application.

So, let me throw one out there and see what you "think." Believing is *how* you think and most importantly where you think *from*.

> **Rhema Code Truth: "Believing" is measured by where you think from and how that affects your actions and attitudes.**

Believing is not only tied to right thinking but "authentic" believing is where you think *from*. Thinking from His world leads to actions and attitudes that line up with that reality. It's not about moral rightness. It's about thinking His heart.

A true believer is one who centers his or her thinking from His world. Jesus made the grand offer to us to enter into His world—the Kingdom—and to change the way we think, including changing where we think from, and to have the resulting action of that shift show up in how we live, talk, act, love, etc.

Instead of having no real way of defining for ourselves our level of belief or *beliefism*, this gives us total measuring ability. It puts substance to our "believe."

Have you ever struggled with trying to evaluate where to go in a conversation with someone who defines their position with God by simply saying they are a believer? I mean, where do you go with that?

Instead of settling for some generic answer like, "Yes, I believe in God," the idea of "thinking from His world" and the ensuing actions are a great way to measure if people have fallen into the trap of some mental ascent toward God. Do we believe? Have we truly taken on and incorporated God's core values in everyday life? In other words, do we embrace what is important to Him in an identifiable way? Do we love what He loves; do we do what He does; do we say what He says?

This definition of what it means to believe is also a great tool for believers to help those who are "stuck" in their approach to God. It gives us a resource to help point people in the right direction toward an authentic encounter with God. People will marvel when you share with them a tangible way for them to access Papa's heart.

The Difference Maker

The challenge to this line of thinking is that it leaves no wiggle room for a half-hearted approach to Jesus. When He pulls you into His world He not only gives you a brand new identity, He gives you a whole new realm or world to think from and to act from. If you are an authentic believer you will make an application of His reality in every circumstance and situation in life. God doesn't even make this point optional.

For the "casual believer" (oxymoron) there isn't necessarily any intentional living going on except for the lingering thought of making moral decisions that keep God's judgment at bay. But a true "believer" is always on assignment to accurately represent God's heart to every person he or she comes in contact with. Remember: we are now thinking from His world, and in His world He loves people with a crazy level of love.

Not only does God's great love gift of grace give you and me a new identity, it gives us new perception with a new reality to think from and a new Person to think with.

Integrated thinking

Integrated thinking is the result of renewing our minds and learning to think and live in harmony with God "from" His world.

> **Integrate**: to form, coordinate, or blend into a functioning or unified whole: to unite with something else: to incorporate into a larger unit: to end the segregation of and bring into equal membership; to synchronize.

Several months ago, Lori and I were hosting Todd White over a weekend and in the middle of one of our conversations, Todd commented on how Lori and I were able to finish each other's sentences.

After 32 years of marriage we had come to a place of "integrated" thinking. Our lives are in harmony. We live from the same core values.

Words and actions or declaration and demonstration are the by-product of living in harmony or living with integrated thinking.

Declaration and demonstration are the basic summary of each person's life. What you say and what you do come from how you think and where you think from.

In Jesus' case: He models the marvelous reality of a life synchronized with Father.

In essence, Jesus' life would be defined or summarized by these two statements:
I say what the Father says…
I do what the Father does…

> *I say to you, the Son can do nothing of Himself, but what He sees the Father do; for whatever He does, the Son also does in like manner.* (John 5:19)

> *I do nothing of Myself; but as My Father taught Me.
> . . (John 8:28)*
>
> *. . .whatever I speak , just as the Father has told Me,
> so I speak.* (John 12:50)
>
> *The words that I speak to you I do not speak on My
> own authority; but the Father who dwells in Me does
> the works.* (John 14:10)

In this case the two become one expression and in this expression Jesus transfers His core value to us: amazing harmony with God's heart and God's world.

Integrated thinking and living happens when we identify our trend toward independency and replace it with total and absolute interdependency with Father, Son, and Spirit.

Is there a verse that raises more expectation than this one?

> *Most assuredly, I say to you, he who believes in Me,
> the works that I do he will do also; and greater works
> than these he will do. . .* (John 14:12)

This carryover from Jesus' life is now passed on to us and we love the idea of greater things, but do we get the degree of integration required to live from that reality?

This could be a helpful way to look at this verse and make the "believe" part make more sense:

> *He who believes* = those who think from His world; those who think in harmony with Him.

Jesus is saying to us: as I thought from Papa's world I was modeling for you how to think from my world and in doing so you will duplicate what I did and even more.

He even goes so far as to say, "when you think from my world and ask I will agree with your agreement. . .because you embrace my core values I will empower your request."

> *And whatever you ask in My name, that I will do, that the Father may be glorified in the Son. If you ask anything in My name, I will do it.* (John 14:13-14)

I will do. . . or . . .will I do = one word which includes the idea of "agree and abide," resulting in executing the demand.

Summary of thoughts here: those who align their thinking with God's—not just on the topic at hand but on every topic at all times and take ownership of His world—place a demand on Heaven that God obligates Himself to line up with and partner with to release His goodness into an inferior realm. This is why "to believe" is so interconnected to how we think and where we think from. It starts with getting your "identity" figured out and learning to live in harmony with Jesus from a "condition" as a son or daughter. Believing is thinking from His world and learning to "say and do" with God at all times and in every situation. Believing is taking on His core values as your own and living from them.

When we get this, it will make this next verse, John 14:21, make more sense. You must read it as a "new creation" son or daughter, not as a servant.

> *He who has My commandments and keeps them, it is he who loves Me. And he who loves Me will be loved by My Father, and I will love him and manifest Myself to him.*

Please note the following:

> *". . .has My commandments"* means precepts, heart, ideas.

> The word "command" used here is in a yoking context ["Yoking" means to be enjoined or driven to a life of response by the yoking of your heart and mind. If God doesn't have your heart He will never have your mind. Notice the progression: "he who loves Me keeps My commands. . ." or ". . .he who has My heart will think, act and talk like Me!]—a place of interconnectivity—not at all from a distance as we might use the word in our language. The context of keeping His commands is not measured by simple activity. It also means injunction, or to do, or refrain from doing, a specified act; from the condition of being yoked together.
>
> He who has My commands "and keeps them" [maintains a watch over them or keeps an eye on them] is always vigilant to keep the heart of the Father at the forefront in every situation and circumstance.

It's a wonderful place of ownership and agreement. It's not a duty or an obligation. It's a reality that you have connected with and made your own. It's the life of a believer. As a "believer" we make Heaven, God's world, our own and we live from there now. In Him we think, act, move and have our being. "In Him" includes in His world!

Catch the power of these verses from The Message:

> *What a God we have! And how fortunate we are to have him, this Father of our Master Jesus! Because Jesus was raised from the dead, we've been given a brand-new life and have everything to live for, including a future in heaven—and the future starts now. . .* (I Pet 1:3-4)

You, my friend, are "the next great move of God" and God is ready to move…are you?

Can we just be together, no facade just me
That's why when I'm with you I'm completely free
No strings attached
There's nothing I could say or do
To attain your sweet sweet love for me.

— "Let's Just Stay" by Destiny Schang

CHAPTER FOUR

Complete

"Conditional Theology" or the "Theology of Your Condition"

Anything less than a full-fledged, radical and complete inner transformation by the power of God's "great love sacrifice" at conversion is a recipe for an awkward and frustrating "Christian experience."

The wonder of our new birth in Christ is stunning. We call it a miracle, but do we realize how miraculous it really is? He didn't give us a fresh start; He gave us a brand new start! He didn't wipe your slate clean; He threw away the slate! If you are in Him, you are an amazing and completely new creation!

Why is it that many who call themselves "Christian," struggle throughout their lives trying to find meaning, satisfaction and a sense of well being, often leaving in their wake an ugly legacy of pain and disappointment? Many settle for a "someday in the future;" i.e., heaven—approach to anything resembling contentment or happiness!

What is nagging at their core that causes such dissatisfaction, often resulting in shattered lives, broken homes and marriages, leaving very little distinction between Christian and non-Christian people?

What is it that causes people to keep questioning their salvation, wondering if they are loved and if they measure up or not? What is it that causes that initial passion at conversion to fade away and reduce them to go through the motions of Christianity but live without fire and conviction?

Is the answer more prayer, better church attendance, more bible reading, more sacrifice, less sin? How about more fasting or greater discipline? Surely there must be something missing!

Maybe it's getting rid of the thought that something is missing that's missing?

Maybe the prevailing thought of needing to become better instead of living from "already being better" is thrusting people into an unattainable "pursuit mode" that sounds right but is really counterproductive and in fact an error in thinking, leaving many stuck in a confusing attempt at "serving Jesus."

What does it really mean to experience a born again reality "in" Jesus? What kind of power does the Cross have in a believer's life?

In Him…Complete!

> *…in Him dwells all the fullness of the Godhead bodily; and you are* <u>complete in Him</u>, *who is the head of all principality and power.* (Col 2:9-10)

According to scripture, being "in Him" is a pretty good deal for all believers. It's the "in Him" factor that removes the fight to "get it right" and propels believers into a fabulous journey of discovering who they are in Him—not who they hope to become.

Rhema Code Truth: Because of what Jesus has accomplished inside of us, we are able to "live from" complete rather than "live toward" complete.

To Be or not to Be?

At The Promise we call this the "to Be or not to Be" factor, meaning, do you want to dwell in a living "toward" or living "from" paradigm? We choose to live "from complete" rather than toward completion—understanding "complete" to be a condition not an activity. The condition of "already being complete" is the grace gift God gives believers and it is this "condition" that enables believers to "Be" all the things in scripture God calls us to be.

Every "Be" mandate from God is impossible to facilitate through human effort. There are no levels of "works" that will qualify any "Be" status in the Kingdom.

Jesus tosses out the *"in no way small"* challenge to His followers—to "Be holy for I am holy."

> *He chose us in Him before the foundation of the world, that we should be holy and without blame before Him.* (Eph 1:4)

> *...as He who called you is holy, you also be holy in all your conduct, because it is written, "Be holy, for I am holy."* (I Pet 1:15-16)

> *Therefore, as the elect of God, holy and beloved...* (Col 3:12)

If this is not a nature change that He incorporates into us by His grace then we are all barking up the wrong tree. He didn't say become holy; He said "be holy!" God didn't give such a pointed directive like this as an unattainable goal. It is attainable but only as a supernatural gift through Jesus.

So we choose to "be" versus attempt to become. This approach to His Kingdom changes everything. It changes what we are "living from" and it changes what we are fighting against.

You can't work hard enough to "be holy" or to become holy. Holy is a by-product of receiving and agreeing with our "complete" status in Christ—holy being a "condition" not an activity.

The idea of working towards God is an Old Covenant way of thinking and living, and there seems to be just enough Old Covenant thinking in many Christians that they can't help themselves from attempting to help God out with the process of making their lives more presentable to Him. Even at times we turn good things like prayer and devotions and church life and character building into religious substitutes for an authentic relationship with Him that end up falling into the same category as the man-made rules and regulations that Paul addresses in the second chapter of Colossians:

> *. . .if you died with Christ from the basic principles of the world, why, as though living in the world, do you subject yourselves to regulations — "Do not touch, do not taste, do not handle," which all concern things which perish with the using — according to the commandments and doctrines of men? These things indeed have an appearance of wisdom in self-imposed religion, false humility, and neglect of the body, but are of no value against the indulgence of the flesh.* (Col 2:20-23)

Many of the valuable disciplines of Christianity that are regularly practiced can turn into self-imposed religious forms that are powerless to transform though they seem right and wise when turned into stepping stones toward right standing with God. They can turn from asset to liability at one small yet powerful point of perception: is what Jesus has done for me enough or do I need to add to the process to truly become complete?

Grids, Filters and Paradigms

We use the terms grid, filter and paradigm to help people recognize their process of thinking and to identify why they think the way they do. Every thought that we project into a life application comes from somewhere and is sent out through something. We have a receiving grid and a sending grid. In other words, the concepts that fill our brain are impacted by the way we have been raised and the way we have been taught. Our ideas have also been shaped by the things that have happened to us in the Christian world, by the ideologies we have been presented with and by the values we have allowed leaders and teachers to influence us with.

These thoughts and ideals then become the basis of our receiving and sending mechanisms. What we "grid in" we "grid out." One concern I have for people is having them allow others to influence their "grid" and not even realize it—basically allowing people and circumstances and cultural ideas to think for them instead of thinking for themselves.

The classic example of this is the story of Adam and Eve in the garden being subtly yet aggressively deceived by the serpent as he convinced them of what they didn't have. As this tragic fall from Royalty developed, God asked such a profound and important question to the both of them: "Who told you that you were naked?" A paraphrase of this question could be: "Who influenced your grid?"

Where did this thinking process come from? How did they come to the conclusions that got them into the mess that they found themselves in?

Having a clean grid or filter is so important in our Kingdom journey. We can't afford to have someone or something else think for us. We can't afford to have preconditioned teaching or cultural trends think for us.

A good friend of mine told me this story that illustrates the power of preconditioned thinking. She and her husband were driving past a large cow pasture in the springtime as they had many times over the years and there they were again—hundreds and hundreds of daffodils sprinkled across the landscape of that pasture intermingling with the meandering cows. Many springs previous they has discussed this marvel, for no other pastures in the area were laden with that beautiful spring blanket like this pasture was. In passing, her husband had given her the explanation for this spring splendor: "Someone threw some daffodils onto the pasture, the cows ate them and, "Voilá;" they spread the daffodil seeds throughout the pasture and now we get to enjoy the scenery every year. Thank you hungry cows!

Like clockwork, the daffodils rose to the surface again this spring and my friend was sharing her little personal treasure with a co-worker: the cow eating the flower and passing the seeds theory and all. At the end of the conversation her co-worker said, "Don't daffodils grow from bulbs?" At that point, years of preconditioned thinking came crashing down. She realized that she knew daffodils were a bulb crop yet she had let someone else think for her and had held firmly to her position for years.

The riddle of the flower frenzied pasture was solved when she found out the field used to be a commercial bulb farm before being turned into food for cattle. Her husband still denies telling her the seed story!

One of my close friends was traveling with his family raising support for the great work God was doing through them in Mexico. As they were traveling through Texas, a couple pastoring a church invited them to their home and politely made their pool available to their small children. After about 30 minutes one of the teenage girls that was watching the young children in the pool came running panic-stricken into the house and led the adults to the side of the pool where my friends four-year-old son had been pulled from the pool and was unconscious, blue and not breathing. My friend's wife began mouth to mouth resuscitation on her son as the siren from an oncoming ambulance was blaring in the background. Suddenly the little four-year-old coughed and threw up the water that was in his lungs and began to cry as the color returned to his body. The paramedics then arrived and hurried him to the ambulance. Before leaving for the hospital the paramedics warned the missionary family that even though their son was alive now, depending on the condition of the water that entered his lungs, he could have an intense battle with bacteria that could still cost him his life. They went on to tell the family that many of the people that are revived from drowning accidents lose their lives from infection because of impure water.

After a couple of days in the hospital the young boy was released with a clean bill of health thanks to the purity of the water in the pool. It seems the filtering system saved the boy's life. The filtering system in the pool was in excellent shape and had been regularly maintained producing a bacteria-free environment.

Our need of a clean filtering process can't be overstated—our receiver and sender is at stake. What we allow in must be pure and healthy to our system so that the outcome or outflow is healthy and pure as well.

Which grid do you live from?

This is a question worth asking. Maybe you've never even thought of the question before. Maybe you didn't know there was a question that needed asking. There is! How do you see yourself—complete or incomplete and why? Do you "think" of yourself in a certain way because of pre-conditioned teaching that has done the thinking for you? Or do you "think" from a grid that is in agreement with what God has already done for you?

Is your intake filter on the pure side or does it lean toward impure? In other words, do you take an incomplete position or a complete? Are you still in a fight with your old nature or are you in agreement that the battle's been won on the cross?

Continuing in chapter 2 of the book of Colossians, Paul refers to "the indulgence of the flesh," and speaks clearly to the issue of completeness:

> *...why, as though living in the world, do you subject yourselves to regulations— "Do not touch, do not taste, do not handle," which all concern things which perish with the using—according to the commandments and doctrines of men? These things indeed have an appearance of wisdom in self-imposed religion, false humility, and neglect of the body, but are of no value against the indulgence of the flesh.* (Col 2:20-23)

Indulgence here means the need to be satisfied or fulfilled, and is addressing the inability of anything to fully meet the need of a person who is living in a natural or fallen state of mind.

Jesus is the Need Meeter

A transference of natures is the only cure for a "flesh" problem. In Christ we are "completely" transferred into a different state of being, no longer of a temporal condition, no longer fighting against a sin nature. We are partakers of Jesus' divine nature. He is the ultimate need meeter! He satisfied the requirements of the law and set us free from the law of sin and death:

> *For the law of the Spirit of Christ Jesus has made me free from the law of sin and death. For what the law could not do in that it was weak through the flesh, God did by sending His own Son in the likeness of sinful flesh, on account of sin: He condemned sin in the flesh, that the righteous requirement of the law might be fulfilled in us who do not walk according to the flesh but according to the Spirit. For those who live according to the flesh set their minds on the things of the flesh, but those who live according to the Spirit, the things of the Spirit. For to be carnally minded is death, but to be spiritually minded is life and peace.* (Rom 8:2-6)

A transference of natures does not happen by retraining the mind. To be spiritually minded starts by having a heart transplant. Jesus gives us a new heart—a new condition that enables us to think from "His" world. With the sin issue dealt with, we can now grid or think through a clean filter!

> *. . .may the God of peace Himself sanctify you completely; and may your whole spirit, soul, and body be*

> *preserved blameless at the coming of our Lord Jesus Christ. He who calls you is faithful, who also will do it.* (I Thes 5:23-24)

There are some large words here worthy of taking a look at. . .
- Sanctify: to make holy
- Completely: absolutely perfect, complete to the end
- Preserved: to keep; as under guard
- Blameless: "unblameable" and faultless

These are amazing "condition" words that God gifts us with, and. . .

> *. . .you, who once were alienated and enemies in your mind by wicked works, yet now He has reconciled in the body of His flesh through death, to present you holy, and blameless, and above reproach in His sight.* (Col 1:21-22)

What an amazing thing God has done for us, thoroughly and completely demolishing the hold that darkness had on our lives! We truly belong to our Father in Heaven, and we are His sons and daughters—and all accomplished apart from our own efforts!

From this condition we are able to "set our minds" on the things of the Spirit. In Christ our minds are released from the bondage of a fallen world.

The Resistance: Lack

Webster's Dictionary defines the word "lack" as follows:

- To be deficient.

- To be short or have need of something; to stand in need of; suffer from the absence or deficiency of.

It is a word that has been leveraged against mankind starting in the garden. It is the antithesis of complete. It may be the most slanderous concept thrown in the face of God and into the minds of humans. It is infectious and contagious. It infiltrates, steals, kills and destroys!

I have been amazed at times to see how aggressively people will fight for the right to live from a place of lack in their Christian experience. How dare someone challenge their condition of depravity. "Don't you know I'm a sinner saved by grace?"

After a full hour of teaching on the topic of God's complete work in the heart of believers, while visiting with people, I was putting my things away when a man came up to me red-faced and angry, evidently not hearing any verses or teaching points except the phrase defining the word complete, which included the word "perfect." Perfect being the "complete" work of Christ on the inside of a believer forever changing the "condition" of the heart. He was not leaving the building until he made his point about his personal sin nature and how dare I suggest he was in any way, shape or form "perfect." Realizing the situation was not life threatening, [W*here was Carl when I needed him? Carl, being my neighbor and fellow brother in Christ who is a sniper for a Metro Police Swat Team and who told me he would take a bullet for me if the situation arose, was not around. Carl is also my ex-hunting partner. I came to realize that as long as I hunted with Carl I was never going to get a shot off. I am so glad I have two legs and not four. I would not want Carl hunting me!]* I let my red-faced friend maintain his hold on his theological grid as he echoed the thoughts and layers Old Covenant teaching placed on him over the years by various leaders who reinforced his need to have them help him not fail in life.

I have found it fascinating to hear and see the response of Christians who are bound up by pre-conditioned teaching about their "sinful nature" and have no wiggle room to think from a different paradigm. For some who are severally entrenched in "lack," the suggestion of "perfect" (*which means complete*) is worse than a swear word.

I realize it does present a paradox for many when faced with the truth of how radical the grace of God is. It takes away any excuse for living a substandard spiritual existence and makes no room for turning Christianity into a spectator sport.

I've watched people struggle with the idea of "complete" when they realize what it means to their day-to-day experience as a believer. It's like having the rug pulled out from underneath of you. No longer clamoring for solutions and fixes for lack is like a dog that no longer has fleas. What do I do now? Where do I put my energy and focus? You mean I am now part of the solution? Yes, we turn from being a project to projecting; from being an ongoing "working to get better" person to "projecting" God's world to those around us.

The word "project" means to "present for consideration; to display outwardly." God has done such a great work inside of you that He wants to put you on display for the world to see. If we are going to influence the world in any significant way we have to move from being a project to being on display. The world desperately needs to see what is inside of us!

> *...You're here to be light, bringing out the God-colors in the world. God is not a secret to be kept. We're going public with this, as public as a city on a hill. If I make you light-bearers, you don't think I'm going to hide you under a bucket, do you? I'm putting you on a light stand. Now that I've put you there on a hilltop, on a light stand — shine! Keep open house; be generous with your lives. By opening up to others, you'll prompt people to open up with God, this generous Father in heaven. (Matt 5:14-16 MSG)*

Rhema Code Truth: Our perception of what we are on the inside is what we will display on the outside.

The influence of "incomplete" in the area of relationships:

It is essential that we don't make the mistake of misidentifying what God has done for us as "incomplete." If we don't see what He's done as the total package and live from that complete work, we will feel compelled to add to the process and live in pursuit of what He has already done for us.

If we "pursue complete" everything we connect ourselves to will be evaluated through a grid of "lack." If we see ourselves as anything less than "complete in Him," we will ever be living "from" the status or condition of incomplete or living from lack. This condition then is transferred into and onto everything we connect with. Every activity, event and relationship we are a part of will take on a dimension or characteristic they were never designed for—creating a life of conflict and tension instead of blessing and peace.

Rhema Code Truth: Living from a lack perception will place a burden on all things around us to become part of the solution for our state of "incomplete."

Living from a "lack grid" or a "perception of lack" will place a burden on all things around us to become part of the solution for our state of "incomplete," putting overt pressure on relationships and things to fulfill an inner need they were never meant to fulfill nor are able to.

We, then, will inevitably live in a tension-filled life that is never satisfied as we live from an incomplete grid, consciously or subconsciously, striving to get rid of that nagging sense of inner dissatisfaction.

In relationships this truth is quite evident. We see and listen to love stories that go something like this: "Baby, you complete me" and people fall for it. Instantly the hairline fracture of relationship disaster appears. Leaders and counselors work with couples on a regular basis trying to repair relational problems that often come from a misguided notion that "my spouse" is not doing a good job at meeting my needs—"Don't you know you are supposed to complete me?"

God has pointedly "encouraged" me to stop trying to put a temporary fix on people's relational problems. It's like giving a car a new paint job without removing the rust. It won't be long and the problems will resurface in some way, shape or form. I rarely counsel marriage problems away anymore. I now invest my time empowering Kingdom realities including the "condition of complete" into the hearts of those who haven't dealt with the rust.

We are battling a culture that has taught people to get their needs met. Come to doctor/pastor and see if he or she can make things better; turning the church into a hospital, or a weekly self-help seminar, instead of a gathering of triumphant and victorious people.

It is a fascinating and at times frustrating thing to witness. Couples who desperately want to feel better but don't want to "be" better, trading a permanent condition for a temporary feeling.

Living from lack or an incomplete condition will automatically place those you are relating to into an impossible position of being a resource for an inner state of being they were never meant to fulfill for you! Only Jesus holds that role and He holds it jealously.

Relational "performance" is the backbreaker of what usually starts out relationally with great promise for many couples and for many families. No one means to submit to the oppressive grip of performance-driven relationships and not many look for the antidote in the complete work of the Cross—in Christ's complete overhaul of the human heart.

When the real you truly embraces the magnificent reality that you lack nothing in Christ, you set everyone around you free to enjoy quality relationships—including yourself.

Lori likes to can fruits and vegetables from our garden and orchard during the harvest season. When she has that pressure cooker cranked up on the big burner it reminds me of the relationship pressure many people find themselves in. That canner is so agitated inside that the pressure has those glass jars banging around as the water is beyond boiling. I find myself waiting for the whole thing to bounce off the stove. At times it's even a little scary; the only thing that separates the pressure cooker from being a bomb is the small steam vent on the top of the canner. The whole process of canning is not finished until the timer goes off and we are able to turn the burner off and let the canner cool before removing the lid and taking the jars out.

In the past I found myself temporarily turning the heat down on people's issues, hoping the "stuff" inside would go away. It doesn't. Sooner or later the heat of unmet expectations rises up to the boiling point again and that little "doodad" on top of the vent goes crazy. Taking the lid off is the only real solution to the problem and that's what happens when the full revelation of a brand new and "complete" inner reality is embraced. All the fuss and pressure fades away and His peace comes.

When people catch this truth they are launched into a realm of relational success they have only dreamed of. Often, for the first time in their relationships, they find a freedom to truly love without the pressure to do something they were never intended to do—"complete" their mate or "complete" a family member. Love never works well when it is coated in a "have to" mind set. Love thrives when it finds itself free to "be" in a "get to" paradigm.

> **Rhema Code Truth: Only Jesus holds the key to your heart; allowing anyone else to "complete" you will only end in disappointment!**

Here is the point to all of this: there is a need in the heart of every person on earth that only Jesus can meet. Only He can "complete" you. Attempting to allow anyone else or anything else will only lead to disappointment.

Meagan's story: Upon leaving the hospital where she had been with her mother who was going through treatment for a tumor, Meagan was feeling the emotional drain of the situation and was headed to her car where her husband was waiting for her. In Meagan's mind this was her time for some hugs, kisses and moral support. She was in need of her Steve-fix. When she arrived at the car she quickly opened the door and melted into the seat while giving Steve the details. Steve however was engrossed in a game on Meagan's i-phone that had kept him comfortably occupied while patiently waiting for the return of his wife from this lengthy; yet appropriate, time with her Mom.

It was at this point that Meagan leaned into her "are you kidding me" mode and was about to give Steve a "clue" on missing a chance to meet the needs of his emotionally drained wife. Before she could open her mouth and plead her case, she heard the still small voice of her pastor (me) reminding her that Jesus was waiting for her to cast her cares on Him and that He would do a lot better job meeting her needs than Steve would anyway; not to mention how much better the rest of their day together would be if she lifted the expectation off Steve and allowed their relationship to thrive in a "from" condition. With a quiet exhale Meagan came into agreement with the "Need Meeter" and found a place of rest that only God can give and was spared a potentially rugged relational moment.

If we view what God has done on the inside of us as only a partial fix instead of the full meal deal, we will continue to search for the full deal maker and that full deal maker will come in all sorts of shapes and sizes, colors and forms and will always fall short in resolving your inner conflict.

It pains me to hear people confess that they are "fighting their sin nature" as if that is some sort of humble God-honoring statement. What it really is, is a mindset that sets people up for many relationship challenges. It subconsciously puts blame on God for not getting the job done and it puts pressure on everyone and everything else to supplement the process.

> **Rhema Code Truth (Relationship Success Key): Your ability to enjoy and flourish in loving, quality relationships is directly connected to your personal understanding and "yieldedness" to the complete work of Christ within you.**

Have you ever noticed people's tendency to embrace God's heart for their lives when the sea of life is calm? For example, when it comes to the complete work of Christ in the individual, it's generally much easier to live in the affirmative of that truth when no natural circumstance is challenging a person's well-being.

I love to help people realize how powerful they are in Christ, but the reality of that truth only manifests itself if people live "from complete." One of our greatest positions of power in Jesus is our ability to disempower anything or anyone from having more power and influence over our lives than He does.

In relationships it is critical to keep Jesus at the core of your "condition" of "complete." If you don't, the first time someone lets you down or hurts you, you are at that person's mercy when it comes to your emotional and inner well being. Again and again I've watched this scenario unfold. A person comes along my path in emotional distress over a relationship glitch. I understand their pain; that is to be expected, but, how much influence do we give someone else's weirdness. To what degree do we allow ourselves to spiral down over circumstances or people issues?

My job description becomes very simple and obvious in moments like that. I point them back to the core issues—the reality of "who they are" and "what's inside of them" and "who or what are they going to make more powerful"— that which is "happening around them" or "that which is within them?"

If we don't settle the issue of where we really resource from, we will never walk in a place of "peace that passes understanding; a place that guards our heart in Christ Jesus."

Who do we make more powerful: Jesus, who "completes" us; or people, places, things, jobs, stuff, money, opinions, the past?

The war against your complete condition in Christ is waging every second of your life as darkness tries to pull you back into its sinister grip, using things and people to convince you that you still lack.

We can memorize scripture until we are blue in the face and have gained no ground if we don't embrace this core issue of what the work of the Cross has accomplished in us.

Complete is an "Inner Man" issue

God cares so much for you that He will not allow anyone or anything to take His place in your life. He won't allow His prize possession to be short changed. He does inside of you what no person or power can do! Let's look at scripture and see what God says about Himself and the real you—the you on the inside:

> *For this reason I bow my knees to the Father of our Lord Jesus Christ, from whom the whole family in heaven and earth is named, that He would grant you, according to the riches of His glory, to be strengthened with might through His Spirit in the inner man, that Christ may dwell in your hearts through faith; that you, being rooted and grounded in love, may be able to comprehend with all the saints what is the width and length and depth and height—to know the love of Christ which passes knowledge; that you may be filled with all the fullness of God. Now to Him who is able to do exceedingly abundantly above all that we ask or think, according to the power that works in us.* (Eph 3:14-20)

Listen to this verse out of the Amplified Bible from I Pet 1:23:

> *You have been regenerated (born again), not from a mortal origin (natural seed), but from one that is immortal by the ever living and lasting Word of God.*

And one more amazing verse:

> *Now may the God of peace, [Who is the Author and the Giver of peace], Who brought again from among the dead our Lord Jesus, that great Shepherd of the sheep, by the blood [that sealed, ratified] the everlasting agreement (covenant, testament), Strengthen (complete, perfect) and make you what you ought to be and equip you with everything good that you may carry out His will; [while He Himself] works in you and accomplishes that which is pleasing in His sight, through Jesus Christ. . .* (Heb 13:20-21 AMP)

What God does through Jesus on the inside of each believing heart is absolutely incredible. It's a masterpiece—a work of art—"completely" amazing! Jesus establishes a transformation on the inside of man that is so pure and whole that He puts His name on it. Jesus is the artist and you are the masterpiece!

Living from the inside out

Learning to live from the inside out is such a paradigm shifter. I marvel at the competing responses this truth gets. It is fascinating…that's right, fascinating! I never stop being fascinated by the degree of influence Kingdom truth has on people, both positive and negative. If people are hungry to know God in a personal way—positive. If people lean toward being religious—usually negative. I've heard groans and gasps coming from the same group while releasing Kingdom revelation. I've watched people's faces light up like a Christmas tree at the awakening of who they really are in Christ, and I've watched people stomp away mad when some "sacred cow" truth is being challenged in their mind. What's fascinating to me is that both kinds of individuals are genuinely sincere in their motivation.

In "living from the inside out," it is paramount that we separate the inner man from the shell we call a body, including the gray matter between our ears that we call our brain. As previously stated—the real you is on the inside—the you that is eternal.

When you are born again, you are not only a new creation/creature, you are a new species with a new bloodline and a new Papa and God takes it personal when we see ourselves through the wrong lens or grid.

"It is so important to evaluate accurately which 'you' you are referring to when you refer to YOU!"

The inner man is an identity issue. When you evaluate you, which you are you referring to? When you ask someone how they are doing, the normal response is usually based on the person's emotional or physical condition. This is typically influenced by what is naturally transpiring around them or to them. Rarely does a person think of themselves from the inside out. If I am an outside thinking person, I will adopt that perspective as the grid that I analyze my state of being from. If things are going well around me or if I am feeling well physically then my response to the question will be in the affirmative.

If I am an outside thinker this will also be the grid from which I incorporate scriptural truth. When I limit my perspective to a natural mindset, I automatically place a restraining order on certain truth—releasing the ever predictable "yah buts and what abouts?" "Hey man, you don't know me. I can't possibly be complete, let alone perfect." People don't mean to, but they often allow what's happening around them and/or to them to define them. This thought process seems to prevail among many believers—I am a Christian in word yet a product of my environment.

It's no wonder that we are tempted to place such identity emphasis on the physical part of us. Without a firm grasp on your inner man identity it is normal and even understandable how people fall into the trap of placing such emphasis on what we see in the mirror:
- We feed it…
- We cloth it…
- We feel from it…
- We take care of it…
- We have nerve endings that remind us how alive it is…
- People see us in it…
- People see us perform in it…
- We look at people and evaluate them from it…
- Trends and styles are continually promoted from it…
- We display it…
- We applaud it…

- We pamper it…
- We abuse it…

The natural body of mankind dominates our thinking and our activities. Pastors and leaders can be the most notorious resisters of identifying people from the inside out—often from preconditioned instruction they've received in their training: "Don't you know what the scripture says…'no man is good, no not one!'" That is true. Pre-Christ and apart from Christ and the Divine nature that transforms us, no man is good. Post Christ! Everything shifts.

The body of Christ is not at the mercy of how well they are "doing" or acting or performing or feeling. We are no longer a part of a fallen evaluation system and our Father in Heaven is not looking down on us waiting to record our mistakes and failures to define our level of completeness or whether we are getting closer to that "without spot or wrinkle" thing. This is one of the reasons that I warn people not to trade intimacy for devotions. Devotional activity can be a dangerous trade-off for an authentic relationship with the Holy Spirit because devotions tend to lean toward performance. Then the quality of our walk with God can easily become measured by what we are doing rather than by who we are in Jesus.

Rhema Code Truth: Complete is a state of being—a "condition" that we learn to live "from" as we walk in the revelation of how amazing God is and how amazing He has made us.

Rhema Code Truth: That which we live "from vs. towards" defines us.

...defines us!

Living in the Kingdom involves a new way of thinking—a new perspective—with heightened perception. We learn to think from above. Again it's why we use the word perception interchangeably with the word faith. How is your faith? How is your perception?

Once you are born again and have a new identity that resides and resonates on the inside of you, you also have a new perception available should you choose it.

In Gal 2:20, Paul makes the transformation crystal clear. This is my paraphrase of that verse:

> *. . .the old me is now dead. . .it no longer lives because of Christ. The new me that now lives in this body lives in a brand new state of perception/faith established and founded in Jesus the Son of God!*
>
> *And because of my new found perception/faith, I no longer define/regard anyone according to the outside/exterior, , ,including Jesus and myself.* (2 Cor 5:16)

In Christ and in the Kingdom we are looking through a different lens!

You have got to read these next verses:

> *. . .don't you see that we don't owe this old do-it-yourself life one red cent. There's nothing in it for us, nothing at all. The best thing to do is give it a decent burial and get on with your new life. God's Spirit beckons. There are things to do and places to go! This resurrection life you received from God is not a timid, grave-tending life. It's adventurously expectant, greet-*

> *ing God with a childlike "What's next, Papa?" God's Spirit touches our spirits and confirms who we really are. We know who he is, and we know who we are: Father and children.* (Rom 8:12-16 MSG)

Talk about crazy good! What a deal! We get born again into a reality of expectancy! Things to do and places to go! At The Promise we express core values with slogans, statements and "power points" to help create and maintain the culture we want to live from.

One of our power points that defines what we live for is our four points of encounter with God. It's at the core of all we impart and do.

The Four Points we live from:

Intimacy—our beautiful love relationship with Papa
Identity—the reality of who we are in Him
Inheritance—the wonder of what He gives us
Influence—our privilege of giving Him away

These are the fabulous benefits of the complete work of Jesus inside of those who believe. Anything less than a complete and pure inner condition through Christ's great sacrifice attacks the very heart of these core values. We were made to walk fully and completely in all of these "power points" at conversion. It was never God's intention for us to make these core realities to be goals to shoot for, yet we do this if we live in a paradigm that insists on projecting a spirit and teaching of lack onto the body of Christ!

Spirit of Abortion

It was another one of those moments when the Holy Spirit began to speak to me in my office: "There is a spirit of abortion on the church!" "What does that mean?" "Whatever is happening in society is a direct reflection of what is happening in the church."

> **Rhema Code Truth: When the Church devalues the completeness of spiritual conception, the world will devalue the completeness of natural conception!**

My thought: "Wow!" My question: "How far does that principle reach?" God's answer, "Across the board, but we'll get to that later."

This conversation led to a stunning series of insights and spiritual warfare strategies that have helped develop our leadership paradigm and core values at The Promise. I believe God is making a shift in the thinking of church leaders, sharpening their prophetic focus and redirecting points of emphasis in this journey of leading from peripheral areas onto crucial effective areas that need to be strengthened.

Shaping Culture

We can't be effective in shaping culture if our inner culture is marred by lack. What we are on the inside, we will project to those around us. If our grid is not clean, our world view will be directly influenced by our inner view. In other words, if we live as if we are still dirty, we will live as if we are still dirty! If we buy into the lie that we are still prone to sin we will still be prone to sin.

No matter how passionate we are as leaders in promoting an obligation to change society, we will only be as successful at it as we are at changing people's perception of their inner condition at conversion.

We are spending a lot of energy on things that are symptoms and not the problem. Many of the social evils facing society that the Church wars against are often a byproduct of poor stewardship of truth on the part of the Church in general. If we want to be a part of the solution to resolve social ills, we must stop contributing to them! Let me explain before you tune me out.

When I shared this prophetic thought with The Promise Family, I simply started out by saying what the Holy Spirit said to me, "There is a spirit of abortion on the Church"(meaning the Church in general). I could tell by their reaction to the opening statement that all they heard was the word abortion. They signaled unanimous agreement that abortion is not a good thing via their nonverbal language. I began to explain what God was saying through this thought and how it ties into the revelation of God's complete work inside of us by His grace.

When the Church maintains and teaches an incomplete view of the work of grace and promotes a performance-based approach toward a someday in the future condition of approval by God, it becomes the seedbed for a pro-abortion spirit. It devalues the life of a fetus, declaring that the fetus is incomplete until there is some further action or activity. I know this is strong language but here is what God said about this issue: until we get our understanding in line with His and stop arguing with Him and discrediting what He has done in us at the cross, we will have no significant breakthrough against the evils of abortion in society!

> **Rhema Code Truth: Social reform will be inspired by a theological reform of the "complete" work of grace in the heart of man.**

Is it possible that we are contributing to the moral decline of society and the increase of social ills by our poor understanding of the complete work of grace at the cross?

Until we stop placing a load of guilt on the body of Christ to measure up and become something that they already are by His grace, we will continue to contribute to the calamity of the world's devaluing of life and we will keep the awesome wonder of what God has done hidden in the spiritual womb until some ambiguous day in the future.

Rhema Code Truth: When we devalue the power of conception, so does the world!

When we devalue the power of conception so does the world! When we have to see an external demonstration or manifestation to prove value—so does the world!

When God says 'be holy' He is referring to a "condition" that only He can create and we are called to live from that reality. What a gift and what an honor it is to live from that reality…to "be holy" on the inside and to live from that great revelation on the outside… no longer striving to become something that we could never become by our own effort if we had a hundred life times.

It kills me to watch people live as if they are still in the womb and of no real value, working toward that day when they will finally be presentable to God. As if they could ever live such an error-free life in thought, deed and devotion to change the condition of their sinful nature and finally be pleasing to the Lord.

The Scripture in Heb 11:6 is clear on this point, *"Without faith it is impossible to please God."* Without an accurate perception of what God has done inside of you and accurately assessing your new identity in Christ it is impossible to please God.

This place of pleasing God is not an activity. It's a condition that requires faith or perception. To be fully accepted and well pleasing to the Father it requires agreeing with His assessment of you. He is pleased when we lean into who He is and who we are in Him. Everything we do after that is from that context.

Lori and I never measure our level of love and pleasure for our kids by what they do. We even refrain from saying "good job" to them in any context that would make them think we are evaluating them by what they do. Our son and daughter know who they are. They never have to prove themselves or measure up to some standard of qualification. They are free to excel "from" instead of forever trying to measure up in a "towards" grid.

Blameless and Unaccusable

We live in a world of suspicion and accusation. It's the language of darkness. People are so bombarded by accusation that it becomes hard to hear the truth—to hear the good news. Because of a darkened view of God's unconditional love for us, people live in the fear of rejection. This fear is cultivated by bad theology that paralyzes the body of Christ.

> **Rhema Code Truth: Your ability to flourish supernaturally is directly connected to your perception of how God views you.**

Here is His view of those who belong to Him through Christ:
- Blameless: 2 Pet 3:14
- Innocent: Philip 2:15
- Irreproachable: Col 1:22
- Faultless: 1 Thes 5:22
- Unblameable: 1 Cor 1:8
- Unaccusable: 1 Cor 1:8

Each of these conditions as seen in scripture are requisites to a supernatural lifestyle. If we live in fear of consequences and rejection from God for our actions we will be battling that fear and never effectively move into the action part of our calling and birthright.

Your identity as a son or daughter of God dictates the condition of your heart which directly influences the level of supernatural activity you live in.

The gloomy news of how bad someone is and how far they have to go, and how much they need to do, and how prone they are to failure is poor incentive toward a quality relationship with God and creates a fuzzy self-portrait.

Several years ago I had some high country white pine logs given to me which my son Casey and I made into a nice bed. We worked together on it with the idea of it going in Casey's bedroom when he got married. It turned out to be a beautiful bed! I was so sorry it didn't fit into Casey and Ashley's bedroom and had to be stored in Lori's and my bedroom.

Left over from the project was a five foot piece of white pine. I cut it in half and rough cut each piece into the shape of cones to someday be carved into decorative trees. Those two pieces of wood have been outside mocking me for the last handful of years. Nearly every time I walk by them I hear them taunting me with accusation of failure, "You can't carve us, what if you mess up?" One day I even went as far as throwing them on a burn pile, for some reason thinking it would be easier to burn them up and get them out of my sight rather than be plagued with possibilities unfulfilled. Adding to the pressure, were the subtle hints Lori was making about getting those stupid chunks of wood out of sight (I think they were talking to her as well!). I finally realized how ridiculous this whole journey was becoming and walked by them for the last time on my way to get the chain saw and close their mouths for good.

Somehow the underlying thoughts of failure and rejection had turned into a weird sense of fear that had stopped my creative drive before the engine could even get started. I flipped the switch to "on" and pulled the starter cord and resolved in my heart to never let the fear of failing ever make me miss out on the amazing opportunities God has for my life, no matter how small or great. The trees turned out fine The little blocks of wood were never the issue. I just had to get my perception in line with Papa's. His love for me isn't influenced by what I do or don't do! I can't do enough things right to get Him to love me more, and I can't do enough things wrong to get Him to love me less.

> **Rhema Code Truth: Obedience is not an activity; it's a condition of agreement with God's heart that launches us into activity.**

Did you know that the heartbeat of obedience is not an activity? It's a condition of agreement and alignment with what God says that launches us into activity. When He is saying "obey," He is saying, will you align your thinking with mine so we can get this job done? It was never meant to be a leverage point to get us "somewhere" or a tool of measurement of our spiritual progress. Obedience is a healthy "perception" of living in agreement with the heart of God.

The word "obey" comes from the idea of agree, trust, yield; to rely by inward certainty; to make a friend. To obey is to believe!

The proposed action of disobedience is rooted in a condition problem or a perception problem—not an activity problem. To disobey is unbelief! Disobedience is unbelief integrated with a faithless and faulty perception.

Unbelief or disobedience is saying to God that He is not enough and you need something He can't provide.

What is at the heart of obedience? Identity! As a son, I am completely and competently whole and without lack. I am in need of nothing outside of His sufficiency. Therefore I can believe what He did "to me," and I can believe what He can do "through me."

> **Rhema Code Truth: A person can keep all the rules and be in open rebellion toward God.**

Obedience is not rule keeping and performing.
Obedience is agreeing...it's "being."

Reveling in rule keeping and performing does not equate into an accurate representation of Jesus on earth.

Doing is essential; but, if we get doing out of context it can become one of our worst enemies.

Which comes first—the heart or the act? Not long ago the Holy Spirit took me back to spiritual first grade to help me see how important it is to go beyond having an idea to owning an idea. It's one thing to teach something, it's another to possess it.

In the course of my journey I have five specific things I ask the Lord for every day. One of those things is: "Lord Jesus, empower me to empower people." In response to that daily prayer the Holy Spirit had been putting some things on my heart to do, and in conversation with Him I said, "I can't do that!" His reply was "Gotcha!" He had caught me in a mindset of disobedience. I was responding from "lack" instead of "complete." I want you to notice that I hadn't done anything wrong activity-wise; I had simply resisted a condition. Resisting "complete" led to my unbelieving heart. I had let my mind wander to the point that I was evaluating God's desire for my life from my old reality that was measuring the task at hand from what the natural man could do or not do.

The Holy Spirit made His point and I quickly adjusted my perception. I had made the mistake of resourcing from an inferior condition!

Rhema Code Truth: Lack thinking is identifying yourself from an old man paradigm.

God wants us to approach every situation and circumstance from "the condition of obedience" first and then let the power of agreeing with Him be manifest in our actions. The challenge for many is the personalization of obedience as a condition instead of the misleading idea of a measurable activity. It's generally more popular to lean into a list of things we are supposed to do than it is to live from the condition of something.

The clarity of our Kingdom journey will increase exponentially when we make the shift to living from the "condition" of being complete rather than from the "destination" of complete. I pray the things that have been empowered in your life through wrong teaching and thinking will fall away swiftly as your perception comes into alignment with God's word and heart for your life. We tell our people regularly, "You are amazing!" That's right. . ."Completely amazing!"

If I could see the way you see me
Would I know that with one word from my mouth
The mountain would fall to the sea
If I could see the way you see me
Would I see a heart ablaze with a fire waiting to spread

If I could see the way you see me
Standing tall in a field of giants
One by one they would fall to their knees
If I could see the way you see me
The dark of the night would be scattered by light
With the power that came from my mouth

— "The Way You See Me" by Destiny Schang

CHAPTER FIVE

Faith Equals Perception

I remember watching game shows on TV as a kid and the game show host making this statement of consolation to the contestants who lost and were heading home, "And as a parting gift. . ." This was their polite way of saying, "see ya, loser."

I always felt bad for them as they walked away from their dream of riches and fame. I guess a parting gift was better than nothing.

What does a "parting gift" mean anyway? The more I think about that phrase, the less I like it! "A parting gift." Is it saying, "You're not welcome here anymore?" "Get your coat, what's your hurry?" It doesn't seem to leave the recipient any options.

In hindsight I think I received a "parting gift" once. When I graduated from high school my parents threw me a party with friends and family and gave me a nice set of luggage as a "graduation gift." At the time I didn't track quite as fast as I do now and I missed the "parting gift" message. It wasn't until I was given a key to my apartment a few months later that I "got it." There was no animosity. It was simply, "We love you. It's time for you to grow up. Here's your new address!"

It all worked out fine, and I'll never forget my moving odyssey that followed that first move. Over the span of about 18 months, I moved six times. It doesn't seem like that big of a deal for a young single guy to pack up and move, but that many times in that short of a time span was bordering on ridiculous. I stopped unpacking most of my stuff. I was literally having a hard time keeping track of my address. If I found myself driving absent-mindedly, I would end up at the wrong house or apartment thinking I was going "home." Or more accurately, not thinking, but assuming I knew where I lived only to find myself staring at a building that no longer housed me. It's a good thing it was a small town! My recovery time was fairly short.

In the Kingdom we have a new address that doesn't change. According to scripture, at conversion we inherit a new state of residency. As stated in Phil. 3:20, we become citizens of a new reality. . .

> . . .*our citizenship is in heaven.*

This is one move that doesn't require packing your bags, though it does mean getting rid of your "baggage." The baggage I am referring to is the faulty line of thinking that comes from the old neighborhood. Our new address gives us a new angle on life—a new way of "looking" at things. We are now looking from above downward (God's perspective) instead of from below upward.

According to Jesus we are no longer in debt to, or participants in, the pageantry of earthly living. In John 17:16 Jesus makes a profound statement in referring to those who belong to Him:

> *They are not of the world, just as I am not of the world.*

And the leverage we have against the onslaught of this world's quest to get us to keep "driving" to the wrong address is our faith!

> *For whatever is born of God overcomes the world. And this is the victory that has overcome the world— our faith.* (I Jn 5:4)

Faith is certainly the rack that we hang our hat on. It is the substance that gives us the ability to see or perceive accurately.

Rhema Code Truth: Faith = Perception

We use the word "perception" as an interchangeable word for "faith." Connecting these two key words together has been a great help in putting manageable substance to the heart of faith. Faith is such a big word with so many possibilities and ideas that it can be a bit intimidating when we try to wrap our minds around it. How does one even apply "faith" to their life? We've been told that to have faith is to believe! I agree with that idea wholeheartedly, but what does that really mean? If I really have faith I must "really" believe? How do I get more faith and what does that look like? Okay, faith comes by hearing the Word—and what does that look like? The whole concept of "faith" can easily be generalized to such a point of ambiguity that it can lose its power and "now" application in our lives.

I want people to walk in faith, but I don't want them to jump on the treadmill of self-effort and works in an attempt to muster up something that resembles faith or takes the place of faith.

The core of faith is seeing from a different perspective. In faith's case, the perspective is God's—seeing life from God's perspective or from His world. In our case, to live in faith is to live from an unseen reality yet perceiving the unseen as superior to that which the natural eye sees.

Please don't miss the last paragraph. Go ahead and read it a few times and let it sink in!

> **Rhema Code Truth: It is imperative that we make the unseen realm more influential than that which we can see!**

To look right in the face of a fallen world and see beyond its limitations is the fabulous offer of faith that Jesus died to give us. His greatest act of contradicting this temporal reality was to break the power of death and the grave by rising from its grip.

The resurrection of Jesus was a very radical act that carries with it radical implications...

The resurrection of Jesus was a very radical act that carries with it radical implications, designed by God to take you and me on an amazing journey of defying the laws that govern this fallen world. The call into His Kingdom is a call into a superior realm that offers life-altering potential to all who "see" or live by faith. No wonder the Apostle Paul made such a strong point to the church in Ephesus upon hearing of their "faith" when he prayed for the eyes of their understanding to be enlightened:

> *Therefore I also, after I <u>heard of your faith</u> in the Lord Jesus and your love for all the saints, do not cease to give thanks for you, making mention of you in my prayers: that the God of our Lord Jesus Christ, the Father of glory, may give to you the spirit of wisdom and revelation in the knowledge of Him, <u>the eyes of your understanding being enlightened</u>; that you may know what is the hope of His calling, what are the riches of the glory of His inheritance in the saints, and what is the exceeding greatness of His power toward us who believe, according to the working of His mighty power which He worked in Christ when He raised Him from the dead and seated Him at His right hand in the heavenly places, far above all principality and power and might and dominion, and every name that is named, not only in this age but also in that which is to come. And He put all things under His feet, and gave Him to be head over all things to the church, which is His body, the fullness of Him who fills all in all. (Eph 5:15-23)*

Notice here that Paul had heard of their faith and felt compelled to address their perception.

This powerful prayer for these "believers" was to make sure their spiritual perception, their ability to truly "see," was up to par with the position of faith that they had been brought into. In other words, I see you have faith and I want to make sure you experience the full reality of what that means. I want your true understanding to be enlightened—and the word enlightened here means, to be made to see.

The word perception means: observation, awareness, and consciousness; to recognize; the capacity for comprehension.

> *Fight the good fight of faith, lay hold on eternal life, to which you were also called. . . (I Tim 6:12)*

Our fight of faith is a fight of perception, a fight of an accurate assessment of His marvelous reality that trumps this lesser/fallen reality. His reality, which defies logic and limitations, is expressed experientially through our lives, replacing our lack and inability with "God ability."

How's your faith? How's your perception?

Are you seeing things accurately?

This is the core of Paul's prayer in Ephesians 1 and really at the core of his apostolic calling period. To empower people is to bring them to a place of enlightenment or seeing accurately.

In the medical profession there is a condition called "agnosia." Agnosia is from the Greek word that means not-knowing or non-knowledge. Visual agnosia is the inability of the brain to make sense of or make use of some part of otherwise normal visual stimulus. The *Medical Dictionary* defines it this way: the inability to recognize and identify objects or persons despite having knowledge of the characteristics of these objects or persons... even when basic sensory modalities such as vision are intact.

People with this condition are called "apperceptive agnostics." They can see but they lack higher-level visual perception. Simultanagnosia is a syndrome related to apperceptive visual agnosia, a condition where scenes containing multiple objects cannot be interpreted as a whole. Instead patients with simultanagnosia recognize only portions of the scene at one time and fail to describe the overall nature of the scene and comprehend its meaning. An example of this is a blind person given new sight through a miracle or surgery, who is now being able to see but lacks the visual "perception" to connect what they see with any sense of understanding. They now see but can make no sense of it.

In the spirit realm this would describe a person who is born again, having their eye of faith open yet lacking "higher level visual perception"—seeing but not able to see! Though blessed with new found sight, unable to differentiate between spiritual and natural, or lacking the ability to connect understanding or meaning to the things that are being seen from a new paradigm. For some, they are unaware of any kind of perceptual paradigm shift even taking place.

Imagine what that looks like from God's perspective. He commits a radical act of love on behalf of mankind that shifts those who believe into a totally different paradigm, with a whole different set of laws that govern His world, only to have some of His children have their eyes open…sort of.

It's like going to one of those 3-D movies but watching the movie without the special glasses that you wouldn't be caught dead wearing outside of the movie theatre. You are looking at the same screen as the rest of the folks but definitely not seeing what they are seeing. No matter how hard you try you cannot make the images on the screen do what those glasses do to them. You've bought the same tickets. You're sitting in the same seats, eating the same popcorn, but definitely not experiencing the same dynamics as those who are looking through the lens of higher perception.

"If I was the devil…!" I've used that line many times over the years emphasizing key points of interest in the Kingdom and it applies here big time. "If I was the devil…I would work hard at making people, including believers, think that what they are seeing and experiencing in the natural is the 'full meal deal.'" I would do all I could do to reduce their ability to see, if not eliminate, it. I don't think the devil is too concerned about people getting "saved" as long as they don't have the eyes of their understanding opened.

Un-empowered, non-seeing, unknowing believers are not a threat against the schemes of darkness!

Having faith without higher perception (to see from above) is limiting the believer in every area, including the following areas:

Discernment: discernment is the ability to grasp and comprehend what is obscure or hidden; the unseen things.

Power: power is the supernatural ability to "do." Without higher perception we will typically narrow down the application of power to survival instead of Kingdom advancement.

Intentional living: being specific in our activities according to the revelation of the paradigm we live in.

Authority: activating our dominance over darkness rather than passively submitting to what life throws at us.

Relational harmony: impossible to maintain without accurate perception.

Eternal Perspective: living from an eternal mindset rather than a temporal one. In the Kingdom we don't live as subjects of temporal circumstance; we influence the atmosphere around us by living from the unseen.

The cloud of uncertainty is the playing field of darkness. The ploy of the enemy is to dissuade you and me of any sense of clarity concerning our status in Christ and our role as enforcers of a superior Kingdom.

Lori and I live upriver due east of Woodland in the Lewis River Valley. We are up on a south slope overlooking the valley floor with a view of Mt. Hood. We get amazing sunrises from our perch on the hill and many times we will get up in the morning to a sunny view while gazing down on a fog bank that has settled in the valley below us. From our higher perspective, life is sunny and warm. Yet as soon as we leave our home and head to town we encounter a whole new perspective. No longer do we have the benefit of clear vision and life-giving sunshine that we had from our previous higher altitude. Things are now shrouded in gray and the road in front of us is uncertain due to a lack of visibility.

Having faith from a higher perception is critical to our everyday activity in the Kingdom. Without higher perception we will allow the gray perspective of a lower reality to rule our thoughts and actions.

The words in one of the songs my son Casey wrote are profound in expressing this sentiment: "We need to see your face from a higher place."

Not long ago I was talking to a young man who is a youth pastor in a church in a nearby city. In our conversation, I told him he was amazing. He looked at me quizzically and replied, "You don't even know me," and in some self-depreciating tone that I'm sure he learned somewhere in church life, he continued, "I'm just a sinner saved by grace." He walked away with his head down. In a matter of seconds, I was about to address a crowd of people at a memorial service yet my heart was grieved by this seemingly humble train of thought that people buy into. It wasn't the place or the time to address his comments, but I was keenly reminded of the message that is being regularly promoted throughout the body of Christ; and in fact, one I used to promote without knowing better (we're just sinners saved by grace). This mindset propels people into an endless journey of performance while defining themselves as flawed yet thankfully forgiven.

If my children thought of themselves in that context toward me and their mom it would break my heart. To be a healthy life-giving believer we must embrace a higher perception of what it means to be a son or a daughter.

If we remain uncertain and stay oblivious to or get caught up in working toward what already is, we will inevitably waste precious time and energy on things that have already been established. We can't afford to have the church struggling "toward" things that already are! We can't waste more time on hoping for a "better outcome" when God has authorized us to influence the circumstances of life on this planet.

> **Rhema Code Truth: Only "Higher perception" and "intentional living" will advance the Kingdom.**

"To stake a claim" is a term used in the world of mining. The intention of claim staking is to clearly establish the parameters of rights of the miner; i.e., what are the boundaries of my claim or my property?

Federal law specifies that claim boundaries must be distinctly and clearly marked to be readily identifiable. The clarity of the boundary markers is to stop "claim jumpers" from disturbing or violating the established rights of a miner to be about his or her business. A claim jumper is one who illegally occupies property to which another has a legal claim.

The spiritual lesson of staking a claim is obvious. Satan is the claim jumper who tries to cast confusion and delusion over our rights as sons and daughters and render us sightless and confused. We must operate from the place of obvious and with clarity, having our "stakes" in the ground, readily identifiable and firmly established for all to see. We will never live intentionally if we don't see the full picture clearly.

> *. . .the eyes of your understanding being enlightened; that you may know what is the <u>hope of His calling</u>, what are the <u>riches of the glory of His inheritance in</u>*

> *the saints, and what is the <u>exceeding greatness of His power</u> which He worked in Christ when He raised Him from the dead and seated Him at His right hand in the heavenly places, <u>far above all principality and power and might and dominion</u>.* (Eph 1:18-21)

Seeing is knowing, not intellectual knowing but personal knowing. Here is what is at stake as seen in the above verses:

    The magnitude of His calling in your life. . .
    The full reality of your inheritance. . .
    The exceeding greatness of His power toward you. . .
    The stature of your rank in Christ over all things. . .

Our "claim" cannot thrive in obscurity. We must know who we are and what we are authorized to do. We won't function in power if we don't know we are powerful!

According to Col 1:13, *"Jesus has delivered us from the power of darkness."* The word darkness means "obscurity," and obscure means shrouded in or hidden by darkness; not clearly seen or easily distinguished: not readily understood or clearly expressed; relatively unknown; irrelevant.

If we have a faith/perception that looks inwardly and still sees darkness we will be in agreement with an inferior reality that relegates us to a condition and position of irrelevant. That's right. We will be irrelevant when it comes to influencing anything and anyone around us with light. Our degree of perception of what's on the inside will directly impact our level of influence around us.

In essence, He has delivered us from obscurity—from a state of uncertainty, irrelevance and confusion. In Jesus we live a very definable and identifiable life and we are significant and specifically chosen to shine as light to a dark world.

The great news for believers is that in our case, we don't have to stake a claim. Jesus has done it for us. In Him we are "distinctly and clearly marked and readily identifiable" and so is our task at hand. Our job is to live in agreement with the established and clear truth of our rights in the "Claim of the New Covenant." This was the message that Paul was so moved to give, "that the eyes of our understanding would be enlightened," that we would not only be people of faith but people of accurate perception as well. This is the true fight of faith—the fight to maintain accurate perception!

A Conflict of Paradigms

Paradigm means a philosophical or theoretical framework of any kind; side by side patterns, trains of thought or ideas; a blend of thinking and seeing that runs parallel with other thinking and seeing patterns.

Rhema Code Truth: The conflict of paradigms is a war of "natures."

The fight of perception is tied to a paradigm conflict—the conflict of natures. We live in a tug of war between. . .

Light and Darkness
Good and Evil
Spiritual and Natural

These are the central points of two contrasting paradigms. Light, good and spirit are attributes of God's world. Darkness, evil and natural define this temporal fallen world we call life on planet earth.

At The Promise, we don't do altar calls for people to invite Jesus into their hearts in our culture. However, we do encourage people to walk into God's loving invitation into His world. We discourage people from making the mistake of applying Jesus "onto" what they already have going. His offer of new life and a new nature blended with your old nature is like trying to mix oil and water. It just isn't going to happen. This is the mistake that causes many people to label Christians as hypocrites. What is seen as hypocritical is simply people attempting to apply God to their world, like putting on another layer of clothes, hoping that it will get them in better standing with God. Jesus is reaching out to humanity offering entrance into His world that starts off by creating a brand new you—not repairing the old you or improving the old you—a brand new you!

Rhema Code Truth: Jesus is not an antibiotic for your sins. He pronounces a death sentence to your sin nature. He puts to death the sin issue in your heart.

Jesus is our "door" to His world. When we walk through Him, we walk into a reality shift. We move from one kingdom to another, and it is a radical shift to say the least. To get the complete impact of this shift it is a must for us to have a breakthrough in our ability to perceive the "unseen world" as more real than the one we see naturally.

It is possible to be people of faith but be limited to a natural or world-based view—going as far as seeing Jesus as Savior, but no more. Limited to loving the Lord and attending church, they miss out on the fabulous dynamics of "walking in the Spirit" and the powerful revelation of a "mind set on things above" as compared to the natural lens of "things on the earth." They relegate Christianity to a pursuit of moral behavior and guidelines to be observed instead of a powerful expression of Holy Spirit ability being released through those who "see" that every impossible, natural, limitation is an opportunity for God to expose the inferiority of this fallen world.

This is so huge! You and I were created for and with purpose: to be a living expression of contradiction to natural limitations. Our doing so is directly connected to the issue of perception. Do you long to operate in "great faith?" Then you must be a true believer—one who "sees and thinks" from His world!

When Paul admonishes us to shift our thinking to a higher realm in Col 3:2, he is addressing a conceptual framework issue—an ideology issue. Ideology is the complicated web of entrenched ideas that conditions how you think and feel, which in turn dominates your ability to perceive.

Recognizing the reality of ideologies is key to embracing revelation or truth that goes beyond the scope of pre-existing thought. Ideology can also be defined as a belief system or a conceptual framework. Whatever you call them, they are the mental structures that shape our viewpoint.

Typically a belief system or mindset is difficult to change because of the longevity of its development and the determination of the holder of said beliefs to "be right." That's why scripture-based truth must first and foremost be seen as transformational rather than informational. Simply providing information does not sway a belief system. We take information or facts and fit them into frames we already have. If the facts don't line up we're likely to challenge the validity of the facts or dismiss the information and maintain the current belief system we already hold; often fighting for it, even when it's detrimental to our mental, physical or spiritual health.

It can be categorized as "pre-conditioned" thinking and can be so ingrained in a person's thinking that it thinks for them.

This "ideological" thinking manifests itself in all kinds of things we do and say—often resulting in actions that are unexplainable. People do things a certain way because they've always done it that way. People hold to a belief because they've always believed that way.

Along comes God and He challenges every conceptual framework we have and says to us, "I am offering you a new way to think that will take you into another world—mine! I am offering a new paradigm; one that requires faith to live in and heightened perception to resource from."

Let me paraphrase a verse—Heb 11:6—to make a point here:
>...without accurate perception it's impossible to please God.
>...without the ability to see how amazing God is and how amazing you are in Him it's not possible to fully gratify Him.

God is pleased when we fully embrace what He's done in us and to us. It doesn't do anything for Him when believers struggle through life with some odd sense of unworthiness attached to their minds from inaccurate perception.

Why is it so critical to have accurate perception? Because it will directly influence how you live out your Kingdom assignment on earth. How you "see" and where you "see" from will be the difference maker in your journey of living "up" to your full potential as radical, "on fire" sons and daughters of God.

Perception is a seeing word that is the resource center for our actions. Our actions are a direct result of our thinking. Here's a thought on a healthy progression for you and me to live from:

See. Think. Do.

Faith is. . .having a heavenly perception of your "heart condition, leading to a healthy "mind set" launching a supernatural "life style."

Isn't it great that Jesus gave us a "parting gift"—the gift of the Holy Spirit to live inside of us and give us the ability to "see?" With that "parting gift" in my life, I am very comforted!

. . .you've done it, it's finished
My old man is in the grave
It's over, you took back
The keys from the enemy
So I rose, along with you
You made my life brand new

— "It Is Finished" by Casey Schang

CHAPTER SIX

It Is Finished

When the declaration of "It is finished" resounded from that lonely cross standing atop that hill in that monumental moment; what really happened there? What was finished? What had Jesus accomplished when he suffered horribly on behalf of humanity?

Obviously more than can be expressed humanly and more than can be written in one book, but one thing we know that Jesus accomplished on that historical day. He silenced the voice of the accuser!

> **Rhema Code Truth: The leverage of the accuser was broken at Calvary. It was the end of one era and the beginning of another.**

It was the end of an era of hopeless separation between God and the human race due to mankind's sin condition.

It was the beginning of the Era of the Holy Spirit who, rather than being separated from His creation, found a home inside of His new hosts: "believers."

It was the end of the Old Covenant designed to highlight man's sin. It was the beginning of the New Covenant eradicating man's sin:
> Out with the old. . .keying on what man couldn't do. . .
> In with the new. . .doing "for" man what man couldn't do. . .
> From guilty to guiltless. . .
> From condemnation to uncondemnable. . .

From under the law. . .

> *Now we know that whatever the law says, it says to those who are under the law, that every mouth may be stopped, and all the world may become guilty before God. Therefore by the deeds of the law no flesh will be justified in His sight, for by the law is the knowledge of sin.* (Rom 3:19-20)

To under grace. . .

> *For sin shall not have dominion over you, for you are not under law but under grace.* (Rom 6:14)

From sinful...

> *...for all have sinned and fall short of the glory of God.* (Rom 3:23)

To sinless...

> *...our old man was crucified with Him, that the body of sin might be done away with, that we should no longer be slaves of sin. For he who has died has been freed from sin.* (Rom 6:6-7)

Has there been a more dynamic moment in history since the fall of Adam and Eve? Has any action impacted a greater shift since Eden? No! The era of bondage to a fallen nature was over. That amazing sacrifice of love over 2000 years ago still rings true today—It is Finished!

What a reason to celebrate! The Body of Christ should be the happiest people on earth. Captivity has been broken:

> *...if the Son liberates you [makes you free men], then you are really and unquestionably free.* (John 8:36, AMP)

It's a done deal:

> *...the death that He died, He died to sin once for all; but the life that He lives, He lives to God. Likewise you also, reckon yourselves to be dead indeed to sin , but alive to God in Christ Jesus our Lord.* (Rom 6:10)

The word "recon" means to make an accurate assessment of what is true and in this case live from that "conclusion." It means to recognize the reality of your condition in Christ—which is no longer alive to sin.

My dear friend Dan Schiopu is part of our staff at The Promise and is one of the most talented and fine persons I have had the privilege of knowing. His teaching gift is off the charts and one of his teachings is titled, "The Radical Gospel." In this great message Dan goes over a list of "in Him" statements. Here are two of those verses followed by one of Dan's great statements:

> *He chose us in Him before the foundation of the world, that we should be holy and without blame before Him in love. . .* (Eph 1:4)

> *He made Him who knew no sin to be sin for us, that we might become the righteousness of God in Him.* (2 Cor 5:21)

Dan summarizes: "He became as sinful as you were (on the cross) so you can become as righteous as He is!"

What a trade off Jesus makes for us! These two conditions are as opposite as night and day:

> *For as by one man's disobedience many were made sinners, so also by one Man's obedience many will be made righteous.* (Rom 5: 19)

> *. . .you were once darkness, but now you are light in the Lord.* (Eph 5:8)

Which is it—son/daughter or sinner?

In the Kingdom we don't have two Fathers. We don't split time between natures. It's one or the other. Either we are dead to a sin nature or we are not. Either we have a new bloodline or we don't:

> *How shall we who died to sin live any longer in it?* (Rom 6:2)

Who's your Daddy?

In the Book of John, Jesus said to them:

> *"If God were your Father, you would love Me and respect Me and welcome Me gladly, for I proceeded (came forth) from God [out of His very presence]. I did not even come on My own authority or of My own accord (as self-appointed); but He sent Me.*
>
> *Why do you misunderstand what I say? It is because you are unable to hear what I am saying. [You cannot bear to listen to My message; your ears are shut to My teaching.]*
>
> *You are of your father, the devil, and it is your will to practice the lusts and gratify the desires [which are characteristic] of your father.* (John 8:42-44, AMP)

It really comes down to a war of natures. Jesus wins the war for us, and we decide which one we are going to live from—the old nature whose father is the devil or the New Nature whose Father is God!

A New Species

In Christ we have a new bloodline that transforms us into a "New Species." New Covenant believers are like no believers ever before. By the exercising of our free will to choose to embrace life in Christ in the midst of a fallen reality we become the center of God's ultimate intention. We are His chosen race. We are the ones He planned for from the beginning.

> *. . .you are a chosen generation, a royal priesthood, a holy nation, His own special people, that you may proclaim the praises of Him who called you out of*

> *darkness into His marvelous light; who once were not a people but are now the people of God, who had not obtained mercy but now have obtained mercy.* (I Pet 2:9-10)

What an amazing honor to be His sons and daughters; birthed into a whole new bloodline.

> *. . .knowing that you were not redeemed with corruptible things, like silver or gold, from your aimless conduct received by tradition from your fathers, but with the precious blood of Christ, as of a lamb without blemish and without spot.* (I Pet 1:18-19)

> *. . .having been born again, not of corruptible seed but incorruptible, through the word of God which lives and abides forever.* (I Pet 1:23)

Rhema Code Truth: Jesus is not coming back for a Bride with an identity crisis and His bride is not dirty or ugly.

Without spot or wrinkle is a bloodline benefit that can't be created by natural means. That which is on the outside has no power to influence that which is on the inside. You and I become spotless by what He has done for us!

> *Christ. . . loved the church and gave Himself for her, that He might sanctify and cleanse her with the washing of water by the word, that He might present her to Himself a glorious church, not having spot or wrinkle or any such thing, but that she should be holy and without blemish.* (Eph 5:25-27)

I don't live my life wondering who my natural dad is. I look in the mirror and I see his resemblance. I have his natural DNA. Likewise, I don't spend one second wondering who my Heavenly Father is. I was made in His image, likeness and nature. I have His DNA. When Jesus said if you see me you see my Father, He was talking about His perfect bloodline. Jesus and the Father are one just as you and I in Jesus are one.

> *. . . the glory which You gave Me I have given them, that they may be one just as We are one : I in them, and You in Me; that they may be made perfect in one.* (John 17:22-23)

In Christ we go from eternally flawed to eternally perfect. Our "perfect" is the product of the power of His blood sacrifice that shifts our condition from sinner to saint. Our sainthood is established at conversion. When we are saved, we are no longer accusable. Accusation is only legitimized by a conviction of a violation. When we walk into "believe land," the tag of convict is removed.

> *There is therefore now no condemnation to those who are in Christ Jesus, who do not walk according to the flesh, but according to the Spirit.* (Rom 8:1)

This is not referring to not doing flesh activity; it's referring to living from the condition of Spirit. God is not looking over your shoulder evaluating your performance moment by moment. It's a question of where we are resourcing from and what we are empowering. If we agree with the accuser we empower the accuser. His influence in our lives is limited to our agreement.

> *For the law of the Spirit of life in Christ Jesus has made me free from the law of sin and death.* (Rom 8:2)

> *For what the law could not do in that it was weak through the flesh, God did by sending His own Son in the likeness of sinful flesh, on account of sin : He condemned sin in the flesh, that the righteous requirement of the law might be fulfilled in us who do not walk according to the flesh but according to the Spirit. For those who live according to the flesh set their minds on the things of the flesh, but those who live according to the Spirit, the things of the Spirit.* (Rom 8:3-5)

To have victory in your new identity you must think from it. It's a mindset of agreement with the price Jesus paid to break the power of the old world and the destruction of man's old nature.

Jesus came on the scene to eliminate the substance of accusation, which is the Law. The Law not only highlighted sin in the heart of the individual, it also highlighted sin in the opinions of people one to the other. It literally places "sin" in the airwaves. In the Old Covenant era everything was sin based. In the New Covenant our fight is not against sin or "our old nature." It's a fight of perception. Which world do I live from?

Where are your accusers?

I love this story in John 8:2-6:

> *Now early in the morning He came again into the temple, and all the people came to Him; and He sat down and taught them. Then the scribes and Pharisees brought to Him a woman caught in adultery. And when they had set her in the midst, they said to Him, "Teacher, this woman was caught in adultery, in the very act. Now Moses, in the law, commanded us that such should be stoned. But what do You say?"*

> *This they said, testing Him, that they might have something of which to accuse Him.*

Notice how well-versed the scribes and Pharisees were in a culture of sin. The Law had done its job in their view of others.

> *. . . But Jesus stooped down and wrote on the ground with His finger, as though He did not hear. So when they continued asking Him, He raised Himself up and said to them, "He who is without sin among you, let him throw a stone at her first." And again He stooped down and wrote on the ground. Then those who heard it, being convicted by their conscience, went out one by one, beginning with the oldest even to the last.* (John 8:6-9)

And the Law had done a good job in condemning their own hearts as well.

> *. . .And Jesus was left alone, and the woman standing in the midst. When Jesus had raised Himself up and saw no one but the woman, He said to her, "Woman, where are those accusers of yours? Has no one condemned you?" She said, "No one, Lord." And Jesus said to her, "Neither do I condemn you; go and sin no more."* (John 8:9-11)

Jesus, even before His death, was the destroyer of an "accuser paradigm."

> *. . .For God did not send His Son into the world to condemn the world, but that the world through Him might be saved. He who believes in Him is not condemned.* (John 3:17-18)

Notice that Jesus didn't say to her, "Go and keep the rules." He said to her, "Go and sin no more." Because He had lifted off the spirit of judgment from her life, He released her to move forward in life no longer under the obligation to the law or condemnation and so, free to not sin.

This next verse completes the thought here. Jesus is saying, "If you live in my world you will no longer be under the influence of darkness."

> *Then Jesus spoke to them again, saying, "I am the light of the world. He who follows Me shall not walk in darkness, but have the light of life."* (John 8:12)

Following Jesus as a believer in the light is not an "activity first" concept. It is a condition that as a result has actions consistent with the condition. When Jesus says that those who follow shall not walk in darkness He is not giving a warning about messing up and doing wrong things. He is saying, "If I am in you and you are in me then we have this common denominator—neither one of us has a nature of darkness."

I want to propose something to you. Those in Christianity who resist this way of thinking and fight hard to measure up are the most prone to sin.

Here is the reality of trying to live in the New Covenant from an Old Covenant mindset: "a law keeper is a law breaker." This mindset creates a whole different approach to God than a Kingdom mindset. A law keeper is still nurturing a fallen nature with an expectation of sinning. Any approach to God that includes performance to get "to" Him creates a sense of lack that actually keeps people at an arm's length from Him.

Jesus knew what reaction He would get when He asked the question, *"He who is without sin among you, let him throw a stone at her first."*

Those who keep and enforce the Law are also those who battle with a sin condition. Their own depravity is simply covered over by activity but never eliminated. In Christ our depravity or our sin condition is eliminated!

Below are a few comparisons between Old Covenant Christianity and the Kingdom:

Old Covenant thinkers:
Invite God into their world.
Kingdom Believers:
Respond to God's invitation into His world...
> *From that time Jesus began to preach and to say, "Repent, for the kingdom of heaven is at hand."* (Matt 4:17)

Old Covenant thinkers:
Prefer God at a distance.
Kingdom Believers:
Are passionate for His presence...
> *Repent therefore and be converted, that your sins may be blotted out, so that times of refreshing may come from the presence of the Lord.* (Acts 3:19)

Old Covenant thinkers:
Worship toward His reality.
Kingdom Believers:
Worship "from" His reality...
> *God is Spirit, and those who worship Him must worship in spirit and truth.* (John 4:24)

Old Covenant thinkers:
Strive to become.
Kingdom Believers:
"Be;" they live "from"...
> *...it is written, "Be holy, for I am holy."* (I Pet 1:16)

Old Covenant thinkers:
  Live for works.
Kingdom Believers:
  Live from grace...
   My grace is sufficient for you... (2 Cor 12:9)

Old Covenant thinkers:
  Try to find peace.
Kingdom Believers:
  Live from peace...
   Peace I leave with you, My peace I give to you. (John 14:27)

Old Covenant thinkers:
  Prefer a man to lead.
Kingdom Believers:
  Are led by the Spirit...
   For as many as are led by the Spirit of God, these are sons of God. (Rom 8:14)

Old Covenant thinkers:
  Live with a servant mindset.
Kingdom Believers:
  Are friends with God...
   No longer do I call you servants, for a servant does not know what his master is doing; but I have called you friends. (John 15:15)

Old Covenant thinkers:
  Know about the Lord.
Kingdom Believers:
  Know the Lord...
   ...that I may know Him and the power of His resurrection. (Philip 3:10)

Old Covenant thinkers:
Are structure and system driven.
Kingdom Believers:
Are intimacy and relationally driven...

> *... because you are sons, God has sent forth the Spirit of His Son into your hearts, crying out, "Abba, Father!" Therefore you are no longer a slave but a son.* (Gal 4:6-7)

An Old Covenant mindset is found in a familiar Psalm that we all know and love:

> *Your word I have hidden in my heart, That I might not sin against You.* (Ps 119:11)

This verse is referring to the Law and commands of God's word and in the spirit of the Old Covenant assuming failure and sin. It is applied from a fallen reality and is pointed to activity. This may be contrasted with a New Covenant mindset:

> *For by one offering He has perfected forever those who are being sanctified. But the Holy Spirit also witnesses to us; for after He had said before, "This is the covenant that I will make with them after those days, says the LORD: I will put My laws into their hearts, and in their minds I will write them," then He adds, "Their sins and their lawless deeds I will remember no more."* (Heb 10:14-17)

This is a whole different world where God has redirected His word from the external to the internal and places those who believe into a "condition" that creates purity.

Instead of being under the obligation of the Law to obey the word to measure up which guarantees breaking the rules, New Covenant believers are not required to keep the rules. You can't violate what you are not required to keep.

Rhema Code Truth: A Law Keeper is a Law Breaker.

In Christ there is no Law. It is demolished. There are no rules. We are delivered from obligation. We now live in a "get to" era.

> *... giving thanks to the Father who has qualified us to be partakers of the inheritance of the saints in the light. He has delivered us from the power of darkness and conveyed us into the kingdom of the Son of His love, in whom we have redemption through His blood, the forgiveness of sins.* (Col 1:12)

> *This is the message which we have heard from Him and declare to you, that God is light and in Him is no darkness at all. If we say that we have fellowship with Him, and walk in darkness, we lie and do not practice the truth.* (I Jn 1:5-6)

This again is not first directing our attention to an activity. "Not practicing the truth" means to not be in agreement with the light. It would be consistent with people who say they are believers but have no authentic connection with Jesus or Heaven:

> *But if we walk in the light as He is in the light, we have fellowship with one another, and the blood of Jesus Christ His Son cleanses us from all sin.* (I Jn 1:7)

If you want to break the power of sinful actions in your life, start putting more focus on the supernatural seed line "condition" you have been birthed into and less on what you do or don't do. Your greatest weapon is your birthright. If you are a true believer, you are a pure and spotless child of the King and you don't have a sin nature and you are not prone to failure or sin. You are a "World Changer" living in a NEW ERA! Because…IT IS FINISHED!

Your Spirit fills my heart with love
My soul is moved by your fire
Like the sun I am ablaze
As one I am in you
……..

Your passion drives my destiny
A course set to collide with you
Like the waves upon the shore
As one I am in you
……..

Your majesty reigns in me
Your passion flows through me
Let your glory go
Let your glory go
……..

As your Spirit falls
I'm filled
As the heavens come
We are one.

— "We Are One" by Casey Schang

CHAPTER SEVEN

A Family Culture

One of the key ingredients for raising up powerful and amazing churches is having leaders that understand their role in empowering people with the revelation of their people's amazing and powerful status in Christ. This is what we call leading from an Apostolic mantle—a mantle which creates a supernatural family culture.

An Apostolic mantle includes an empowering mandate—a message of identification clarity for the individual and the church; a message that launches people into a life of ministry that defies impossibilities—a supernatural lifestyle!

To effectively embrace the supernatural ability the Holy Spirit places on us we must accurately recognize what has transpired within us:

God gives us a heads-up in Scripture in the area of how a new way of thinking (repentance) impacts a new way of seeing— *specifically* **seeing ourselves.**

2 Cor 5:16 says, "from now on, we regard no one according to the flesh," *including ourselves.* [Italics mine].

"Regard" means to see, to know, to perceive
"Flesh" means the outward or the body vs. the spirit or soul

To see ourselves accurately we must see ourselves from the inside out—no longer defining ourselves from an external perspective, the outward body, but rather identifying our spirit person.

God wants you and me to know and see ourselves "according to the spirit." There is a direct correlation between the outworking of the miraculous and the perception of "ourselves," especially the "inner man" you—the real you.

A Family Culture

One of our core values at The Promise is living in a Family Culture. A Family Culture is the byproduct of a supernatural culture. A Family Culture is created when people catch the revelation of their own identity in Christ and how that identity integrates their lives with those who they walk with. Remember: we don't go to church. We are the Church; and the Church is a family of supernatural brothers and sisters led by supernatural Papas and Mamas.

When we are totally secure on the inside through the complete work of Grace in our lives, we are able to love without being afraid of each other or without putting undue pressure on each other to meet our needs [see Chapter 4]. The love factor goes through the roof in a Family Culture. It's as if the eyes of our understanding are opened to see what an incredible gift God has given us in each other. Remember, this all starts when you are able to see how incredible you are first. We will always project onto those around us what we see within ourselves.

David's story

It was an epic moment for the nation of Israel. Bondage or freedom was at stake. The Israelites faced a very "large" impossible challenge named Goliath, with no reasonable solution in sight—the very kind of challenge that God seems to thrive on if He can find someone to "thrive" with Him.

Here comes David on the scene with a belly full of God and zero tolerance for anything or anybody that stands in the way of the King and His Kingdom!

Freshly mantled and anointed, David was in the zone, ready to activate the hand of God through his own hand—no hesitation, no plan B. "I know who You are and I know who I am—it's a done deal!" "You and I, Father. Let's go, we've got a giant to kill."

The voice of uncertainty

Unfortunately, David's confidence and enthusiasm were not shared among his family and peers. He was questioned in regard to his motives, experience and ability (1 Samuel 17). David was faced with the same obstacle many of us face in our daily journey—the voice of lack, trying to pull us into the same state of spiritual paralysis it attacks from: "Who do you think you are?" "Where did you get your training?" "You're no match for that giant!" "You're too small." "You're too young." As if their personal assignment is to assassinate the reality of what God has accomplished on the inside of us! *Kill the dreamer. Bring him back to earth. Step back in line with the rest of us you. . .you out of line person.*

Fortunately David ignored the naysayers and the rest is history!

Toward the end of 1 Samuel Chapter 17, we find a couple of key ideas expressed that will help us embrace God's heart in the deal.

> *Then David said to the Philistine, "You come to me with a sword, with a spear, and with a javelin (and by the way. . .not only am I out armed, but you are bigger and stronger than I am.) But I come to you "in the name" of the LORD of hosts, the God of the armies of Israel, whom you have defied. This day the LORD will deliver you into my hand, and I will strike you and take your head from you. And this day I will give the carcasses of the camp of the Philistines to the birds of the air and the wild beasts of the earth, that all the earth may know that there is a God in Israel.* (I Sam 17:45-46)

How can you not love this great comeback of David's? David got it! He had the "it factor"—this man whose life was a prophetic picture of grace, was "called, mantled and anointed." He had all the resources he needed—his partnership with God! He was bearing the name of God!

Rhema Code Truth: One with God is a majority.

> *. . .whatever you do in word or deed, do all in the name of the Lord Jesus. . .* (Col 3:17)

> *...whatever you do or say, let it be as a representative of the Lord Jesus...* (Col 3:17 NLT)

This is not a mandate toward a moral code. These are fighting words; words of empowerment, authorization to employ!

Rhema Code Truth: When you start to personalize your role in advancing the Kingdom, something happens on the inside, something begins to shift.

When you begin to lean into these thoughts and ideas and start to personalize your role in advancing the Kingdom, something happens on the inside, something begins to shift. As was with David, the challenge becomes personal and deep inside; a righteous indignation rises up against every unrighteous affront. No longer do you live in a "What will we do now?" mode, but a "Let's enforce the code" mentality.

> **i.e., Someone or something is coming against the King's mandate, and we (Jesus and I) are not going to stand idle and let it happen.**

I received a phone call from my mom on a Wednesday some months ago. There was obvious concern in her voice, so I knew something was amiss. She said my sister was still in the hospital and things weren't going well at all. The doctors were very concerned because her small and large intestines were not waking up following a surgery she had two weeks earlier. The doctors were stymied; they could find no reason for the problem and even did exploratory surgery to no avail.

This was news to me since I had been informed that she had been released from the hospital days earlier. Upon hearing the news something inside of me began to rise up at the unjustness of the situation. It was as if I began to sense or feel the heart of God on my sister's behalf. With this sense of boldness stirring inside of me I told my mom that I would be up there (a three-hour drive) in the morning and "we" would take care of the situation! I immediately began to appeal to the Lord in a prayer of agreement and made plans for my departure in the morning. This was not a time to be passive and back up into a "what are we going to do now?" mode. I knew God was looking for someone to "thrive" with Him.

In the morning as I was opening the door to my vehicle to start the engine, my cell phone rang. It was my mom asking if we had already prayed. She said at 3 a.m. the problem had been resolved and both intestines were working and not to bother coming up; things are fine. In this case, "thriving" didn't even require being in the same county let alone the same room.

This experience led to a chain reaction of sorts. In our Friday night meeting called "Power Culture," I shared this testimony to our "Friday night" crowd which is usually made up of groups of people from various cities and churches, as well as our own Promise family, who come to get a taste of what God is doing. As usual, the place erupted with a rousing, standing cheer and celebration in honor of the goodness of God being released to a person in need. (We always celebrate the great things God does through and to people, large and small).

I have found that quite often what I walk in, God wants to give away to others, and He was nudging me to release an impartation, a "mantling" so to speak to the people that night. I prayed and released a "healing from a distance" impartation and told them to think of someone close to them who needs to be healed, contact them and that I would look forward to hearing their testimonies.

It didn't take long to get results. A lady who was there that night shared with her husband what had transpired, including the testimony and ensuing impartation. The next day he leaned into the whole thing and called their daughter, a good distance away, who was suffering from an inner ear infection. They talked and prayed on the phone and continued their conversation via texting and by the time they had gone back and forth a few times she was completely healed of the problem.

In the same meeting that Friday night was a lady from the Midwest. She was a teacher at a prominent Bible college who had been in contact with one of her students whose mother was critically ill and fading fast. This woman got on her cell phone and called her student, told her of the long distance healing impartation and released the Kingdom in the sick mother's hospital room a few thousand miles away. I received a text a few days later sharing the miraculous healing story of this dear woman who was hopelessly sick. Instead of dying she had been released to go home with full recovery in sight.

Rhema Code Truth: God will do what seems impossible and He will do it through us.

Then all this assembly shall know that the LORD does not save with sword and spear; for the battle is the LORD's, and He will give you into our hands. (1 Sam 17:47)

We are the weapon that God uses. He doesn't separate His plan, purpose and will from His people.

Like David, we must know who we are and not be moved by the popular opinions of "lack" that try so desperately to get our attention. There is a lot at stake, and we must have our rocks in the bag. In other words, we must be ready—called, mantled, and anointed! We were never meant to watch the game from the sidelines of life. We are "the game!" God revels in doing the impossible, and He wants to do it through you!

This is what an Apostolic Mantle is all about: empowering you to be a World Changer; to take out the Goliath's of life—those seeming impossibilities that can only be canceled out through a person who is willing to "thrive" with God. It's not about what you know. It's all about Who you know and about knowing who you are! It's about agreeing with God in regard to your spirit status vs. defining yourself naturally so He can use you supernaturally.

Repeat after me: "From now on, I will not define myself according to the natural limitations of my body. I choose to agree with my Papa..."

> *Therefore, if anyone is in Christ, he is a new creation; old things have passed away; behold, all things have become new. (2 Cor 5:17)*

Or, to personalize it and put it in my own words:

> *...I am in Christ, therefore I am a new creation; old things have passed away; behold, all things about me have become new.*

There are similarities and there are differences between an Apostolic mantle and a Pastoral mantle. Both are vitally important for the well being of the Body of Christ but both have unique characteristics. In general, one empowers; one nurtures. An Apostolic mantle is tied to a fathering and mothering gift mix. It releases gifting and identity, as compared to the Pastoral mantle which provides care and concern. Both thrive and have the same goal in sight, but they have different applications.

Pastor-led churches have the potential to have an elder brother mentality (like the elder brother who questioned David's heart) as a leadership style: if you do this and this then maybe you'll be ready for the battle. While an Apostolic mantle-led church launches people into *action* through the revelation of their "identity" in Christ.

If a church is not Apostolically-led, there is often a ceiling placed on the supernatural potential of the church family. Moms and Dads believe in their kids while elder brothers and sisters are there to take care of them.

> *. . .members of the household of God, having been built on the foundation of the apostles and prophets, Jesus Christ Himself being the chief cornerstone, in whom the whole building, being fitted together, grows into a holy temple in the Lord, in whom you also are being built together for a dwelling place of God in the Spirit.*(Eph 2:19-22)

Fathers and mothers have a passion for the seed line. They take on the heart of the Heavenly Father who holds the value of the seed as precious. Have you ever witnessed a parent in action when trying to convince those around them how gifted their children are? The Apostolic gift not only believes that but releases that onto people. There is something supernatural that takes place in the hearts of those who lean into an Apostolic Mantle. There is an impartation of Papa's world into the hearts of those who live in a "papa" mantled family.

Pastors don't necessarily have the same gift mix, the same mantle or the same point of view. That's not a slam on pastors; it's a gifting and calling issue. The Apostolic mantle sees the amazing reality of what a person born of the Spirit becomes when Heaven's DNA takes over.

This does not reduce pastoring to an inferior role. It simply helps identify function and actually takes the pressure off certain gift mixes from having to be and do something they were not called to do. We need amazing pastors to care for God's people. Some of the greatest relationships in the body of Christ are between pastors and the people they care for. What we don't need is burned out pastors who are trying to do something they were not called to do and the people in their care "waiting" to be empowered.

You don't have to be an "Apostle" to lead a church family, yet it can really be an asset for Pastors to be in connection with someone who carries that mantle. An Apostolic mantle can be released to a church family through a Pastor in relationship with a person carrying an Apostolic mantle and vise versa.

I propose to you that God is restoring to the Church the role of the Apostle; Moms and Dads with a divine calling on their lives to raise up amazing sons and daughters.

Simply defined, the Apostolic mantle is one that releases identity. That truly is our passion at The Promise. We live to empower people with the fantastic revelation of how amazing they are in Jesus.

In the last days, the Scripture indicates that God will restore the role of the father. I propose to you that God is restoring to the Church the role of the Apostle; moms and dads with a divine calling on their lives to raise up amazing sons and daughters.

Everybody knows how amazing Jesus is. He wants you to know how amazing you are when He takes up residence in your life. Many of you may think you have a long way to go and a lot to learn—not so! Do you know how God used a bunch of unlearned fishermen?—by integrating His life into theirs through the power of Grace. These were men and women who found out their true identity and changed the world. Now it's your turn!

A Spirit of Divorce

The value of a Family Culture came to a pinnacle in my understanding the day God spoke to me about a "spirit of divorce" that was on the Church. Obviously He had my attention and I wanted to know what that meant. Here's what He said: "What we allow within the Church is what begins to plague society. The Church has lost the true meaning of family and has allowed a spirit of divorce to influence her thinking."

As I took that in I began to ask Him for some further insight. Here are a few of my thoughts. Somehow over the years we have lost the value of family in the Church and it has influenced the culture around us. As the Church devalues life and family, so goes society. We are supposed to be the influencers, and I suppose that mantle is released into our culture with both good and bad results. In general the Church seems more concerned with church growth, i.e, numbers, names and noses, than it does with the individual. We are too happy to count people who change from one church to another as church growth. Our measuring rod for success in church growth may need to be evaluated.

Consider the idea of church planting. If a church plant isn't apostolically (supernaturally) influenced, it is susceptible to the "gathering" mentality as its measurement for success. The people themselves become secondary to how many are gathering. The rallying point becomes the numbers, not the content.

Our church culture in general has lost the value of commitment and probably the focal point of it as well. Commit to what: to a cause? to a program? to a building? to going to Church? These things won't sustain commitment. It has to be something more substantial: like people and love; ideas like "I will never leave you or forsake you;" things like "till death do us part."

These days in church life when things don't work out or things don't go our way it's nothing to pack up and move on. What's to hold us there anyway? So-and-so didn't talk to me. Someone looked at me wrong or whatever. I didn't get a chance to display my ministry. No one noticed my giftedness. No one greeted me at the door. These people are unfriendly. They don't offer what my kids need. The list goes on, and Pastors have their own list: these people don't give; they don't attend services; they don't appreciate my ministry, etc. In a Family Culture none of these disgruntled ideas is relevant.

The rotation of people from church to church is a backdrop for every young couple, or old couple, for that matter, that decides they are tired of trying and it's time for a divorce. You haven't met my needs so I'm moving on!

If we want to fix the divorce problem in our world we need to fix us. How do we start? We start by empowering people with their identity in Christ and allow God to grow that revelation from within us to those around us. Does that sound too simple? It isn't rocket science; it's the Kingdom. What transpires within transpires without.

We will never have a Family Culture if we are forever reminded of how far we have to go and how prone we are to sin and failure. A "lack" culture is not a Family Culture. If you don't "think" you are amazing you won't think anyone else is either. If you don't love yourself you won't love anyone else either. You might go through the motions of love but when push comes to shove the real substance rises to the surface.

Rhema Code Truth: Love is only tested when things get testy.

One of the things we teach regularly is: love is only tested when things get testy. Unfortunately, in the revolving door church culture we see so often around us; when things get testy people tend to get going!

Love is supernatural and an authentic expression of love will only surface when love gets a chance to prove itself. When things get testy does your brand of love pass the test?

Catch these verses in Matt 5:43-48 from The Message:

> *"You're familiar with the old written law, 'Love your friend,' and its unwritten companion, 'Hate your enemy.' I'm challenging that. I'm telling you to love your enemies. Let them bring out the best in you, not the worst. When someone gives you a hard time, respond with the energies of prayer, for then you are working out of your true selves, your God-created selves. This is what God does. He gives his best — the sun to warm and the rain to nourish — to everyone, regardless: the good and bad, the nice and nasty. If all you do is love the lovable, do you expect a bonus? Anybody can do that. If you simply say hello to those who greet you, do you expect a medal? Any run-of-the-mill sinner does that.*
>
> *"In a word, what I'm saying is, Grow up. You're kingdom subjects. Now live like it. Live out your God-created identity. Live generously and graciously toward others, the way God lives toward you."*

I am not saying there is never a reason to change churches. There is, but it should be the exception not the rule.

At The Promise we have weekend family reunions and they are fun. We celebrate God and we celebrate each other. We don't have to love each other—we get to!

I won't go up unless your presence goes with me
I'll go so deep into your spirit to know your heart
I'll say what you say, what you do, I will do
Your kingdom come your will be done right here

....

There is no limit to what your power can do through me
Let the wonders of your goodness set the captives free
I know your perfect love cast out all fear
So I declare it to the heavens for all to hear

....

I've been brought into a new covenant
As your spirit brings heaven to earth

....

The impossible is perfect for you
The impossible is perfect for me

— "New Covenant" by Josh Ast

CHAPTER EIGHT

Empowering A Power Culture

Empowering people is making people powerful—powerful on the inside with a demonstration of power on the outside.

What happens when you create a culture that understands power and what to do with it? You have stories like this take place on a regular basis.

Shop Girls...

"I would like to schedule an appointment please," came the request over the phone to the styling salon owned and operated by two of our amazing ladies at The Promise. It was a typical day for Kerry and Kelli in their thriving business—supernaturally typical, that is. The call for an appointment came from a man wanting prayer who was willing to schedule an appointment and pay for the time in order to be prayed for. Who would do that, you might ask? A person in need of a supernatural touch from God would. How would he know to go to a styling salon for prayer? His request was the result of an ongoing release of God's power, presence, and goodness displayed through Kerry and Kelli in their shop over the span of many months. When the power of God is released and people begin to get healed, the people who are in need and the power of the testimony seem to collide.

These two shop girls are examples of lives on display for the world to see, releasing the Kingdom of God in the market place. The list of miracles released through their "shop ministry" is staggering. They carry with them an ongoing testimony of God's goodness transferred through them into human bodies daily and all realized by choosing to live in and from an empowering culture.

> **Rhema Code Truth: We choose to live in and from an "Empowering Culture" instead of a "gathering culture."**

An empowering culture is a culture with a crystal clear understanding of who we are in Christ and what that means in demonstration to a lost and hurting world. People in an empowering culture don't spend time trying to figure out who they are—or put energy into "getting to" a point of being usable in signs and wonders. They live "from" that reality by virtue of the Supernatural influence of the Holy Spirit inside of them. Supernatural is first a condition and then an activity, and it is not caught via a teaching but personally embraced as a product of a transformation of identity.

Rhema Code Truth: When our eyes are opened to the revelation of our supernatural status in Christ, a whole new world of exciting manifestations of God's miraculous power becomes a reality.

In Kerry and Kelli's case and many others as well, the power of God working through them is normal; it's a lifestyle of releasing the reality of an unseen world into the dilemma of a fallen world—partnering with God to be the solution to a devastated planet.

And the stories continue daily. . .

One man came in for a haircut and through a word of knowledge received prayer for a decade-long back ailment. After one of the girls prayed for him he was asked if he felt anything. He replied with a bashful, "Maybe a little." A month went by and he excitedly came back for a trim with the news of a total healing of his debilitating back condition. What he didn't tell the "shop girls" was that when he was originally prayed for he felt the power of God shoot through his entire body like electricity and left with the pain in his back gone on the spot. He had quietly gone home to give it some time to see if it would last. It did!

> **Rhema Code Truth: Learning to yield to His presence is the launching pad of power.**

It has been so interesting to see the manifestation of God's miraculous power released the majority of times through those who are the most comfortable in their skin around God. Those who are free to enjoy intimacy in worship and are able to let God manifest in them and through them. People that are able to learn to yield to His presence without having to figure "things" out seem to carry with them a greater dose of power to give away. When God begins to deal with our inhibitions it seems as if He is opening a conduit for His miraculous power to flow.

Marlee is a great example of learning to yield to "Papa's" love in intimacy and living supernaturally on an everyday basis. Marlee is one of those who seems to relate to the Holy Spirit on a level that we all want but haven't quite got there yet. She has learned to walk in agreement with Papa about who He is and about who she is in Him. The testimonies she carries with her are certainly a compelling argument for the reality of the miraculous and God's desire to release His goodness through His sons and daughters.

One day while in a local supermarket she came in contact with a woman suffering from MS. She politely asked if she could pray for her and then released the blessing of God into this woman's body. It was weeks before she ran into this woman again and this time she greeted a healthy and very happy woman who was no longer suffering from that horrible disease.

I can't count the times Marlee has prayed for people at her job and at various sporting events who have come up to her later with excited testimonies of healing. One day at our local Little League field she prayed for a boy with a freshly broken wrist who was disappointedly out for the remainder of the season. God visited his body miraculously. The young player was back on the field the next game playing catcher and batting and creating quite a stir among the fans who knew about his broken wrist; even to the point of having people come up to Marlee and ask for prayer for their own needs. One time she prayed for one of the girls on our local high school basketball team and God healed an ongoing injury that she had sought treatment for to no avail.

The list of "regular" people from The Promise whom God uses miraculously goes on and on. While ministering in a church in New Mexico, Lori and I took a team of our "regular" people with us to release God's goodness. Most of them were from our School of Supernatural Ministry and they were raring to go. The first night of the conference started out with our "regular" people praying for people with some serious physical needs. One man in particular had hearing aids in both ears and was basically deaf without them. As our team prayed for him God opened his ears and restored his hearing. His wife wept at the display of God's goodness being released through regular people. That night the two of them went out for dinner and he was able to hear things she couldn't hear. Now the husband is hearing aid free and able to minister to people without the hindrance of a hearing disability.

Advancing the Kingdom is not a spectator sport

Often the gap between believing in a core value and enforcing a core value is large. It is one thing to maintain a position or conviction about something. It's a whole different ball game to actually be a part of the advancing, enforcing and promoting process of a core value or truth.

In our "culture" at The Promise, we *empower* people to "be" and to "do;" taking ideas beyond theory into personal application. It can be a challenging new experience for people to embrace their role in the outcome of God's will in a given situation—yet essential for the advancement of God's Kingdom.

It was a normal business day for Don, who works for a major automobile dealership transporting customers while their vehicles are being serviced or repaired.

Don was giving a ride to a regular customer (Tom) who was obviously suffering from a chronic ailment that had been plaguing him for years. In their past conversations they has discussed Tom's condition but never went beyond dialogue. Don had been coming to The Promise for some time and was becoming more aware of the conflict between people's health issues and God's desire to remedy their situation. As they talked Don's attention was turned to God's heart for Tom and His will to bring His world into Tom's circumstance. Don felt an urgency to "get Tom somewhere" so he could be healed. As he began to muster up the courage to address the situation he had thoughts like: *I'll tell him about the Healing room. Maybe he can go there and get some help. Those people pray for the sick and seem to get results. I'll invite him to The Promise; people are always getting healed there.*

At that point the Holy Spirit began to nudge Don with this question: *How about you? How about if I work through you?* His reply went something like this: *You want me to pray? Can I do this?*

Don was facing "the gap;" holding firmly to a conviction, yet struggling with his personal role in the advancement of the cause. For some even the suggestion that God wants to do "things" through them is way out there. Of course for some, the idea that God even does "things" today is way out there!

Don was where many believers are; believing in God's supernatural ability, yet separating themselves from the possibility of being a part of a supernatural solution, i.e., "God is able… but He surely doesn't plan on doing anything amazing through me!"

In the Book of Acts 1:8, the promise of power is defined simply, yet profoundly, as "ability"— supernatural "ability" to do something you cannot do without assistance from the Holy Spirit.

> *...you shall receive power when the Holy Spirit has come upon you...*

What would Don do? Stay in the limited role of simply promoting ideas or become the initiator and transferer of a greater reality? The good news is Don leaned into the process. He prayed for Tom's affliction, laying his hand on Tom and releasing a dose of Heaven into and onto Tom's body, resulting in a mild improvement that led to a complete healing by the time he saw Tom nearly a month later.

What transpired in this real life situation? God was able to release His love and goodness through a person who embraced his role in connecting "Heaven to earth."

We are the equipment

I love this next verse from The Message translation:

> *Jesus called the Twelve to him, and sent them out in pairs. He gave them authority and power to deal with the evil opposition. He sent them off with these instructions: "Don't think you need a lot of extra equipment for this. You are the equipment..."* (Mark 6:7-8 MSG)

In this setting the Twelve are given instruction, authority and power to complete an assignment, modeling for us a New Covenant mandate: "Destroy the works of darkness!"

In our "Be and Do" culture we teach people that embracing their identity (the "Be" part) flows naturally into activity (the "Do" part).

It is a given. Along with our identity, there is always an assignment. Whoever insinuated that living in the Kingdom was boring had no concept of Kingdom identity and activity. Who wants to be Raptured when there is so much to do? When your eyes are open to a Kingdom reality, every single thing looks different. You look at yourself differently, and you look at everything around you differently. It's as if you have been given a whole new lens to look through.

I know I am dating myself, but I can remember when we went from black and white TV to color. Wow, what a change! There was no going back to that "old" format. Everything looked better, more exciting by far and, did you know, that they played football on green grass! No way! (Where I grew up, in Castle Rock, Washington, our high school had a sand football field. They would maintain it with a road grader. That was all I knew until color TV came along.)

We will never do the "do" part well if we can't get a grip on the "be" part. If we listen to the voice of darkness and lack, we will be in an ongoing dog fight that will drain us and render us ineffective.

In the Kingdom, the influence darkness may have on you is not a thing to fear:

> *Then Jesus spoke to them again, saying, "I am the light of the world. He who follows Me shall not walk in darkness.* (John 8:12)
>
> *For you were once darkness, but now you are light in the Lord.* (Eph 5:8)
>
> *Let your light so shine before men. . .* (Matt 5:16)

We are called to influence the world around us with our light. We don't put up with darkness; we turn the light on. We are called out of darkness to expose it—to explode it.

Whenever the power goes off at our house we don't adapt to the darkness and become part of its world, just settling with its influence over us. We always have a game plan. At our house it becomes "candle world." We live out in the country where the wildlife really does roam and when the power goes off it really gets dark—I mean the real thing. We don't have the residual effect of surrounding city lights or the overflow of car lights passing by. We have black—dark! When the power goes off you don't need to wear dark clothes to be hidden. You're in a "can't see my hand in front of my face" state of hidden. When that happens at my house there is an instant unseen yet recognizable stir going on that lasts for about 30 seconds before the first candle is lit. Then the stir becomes a blur as Lori's form becomes visible. It's amazing! The darkness has no chance! I almost feel sorry for it. I don't know where all the candles come from but our house takes on a similarity to Safeco Field at a Seattle Mariner night game. Every time this happens I make a mental note to buy stock in wax.

The power of darkness has no chance against light. The only angle darkness has is to convince the body of Christ that it is still to some degree in darkness. It's this lie that perpetuates a state of non-activity in the church—the subtle thought of, "What do I have to offer to this situation?" It is lack thinking that empowers darkness. I remember talking to a friend of mine one day who held a prominent position in the city. He's a Christian and he made this typical comment to me, "Well, we are just sinners saved by grace." What he was essentially echoing is this dangerous thought that we are saved but still in darkness—still prone toward sin and still battling our fallen nature. That's exactly what the power of darkness would like to talk us into.

I love this verse:

> *. . . For whatever is born of God overcomes the world. And this is the victory that has overcome the world— our faith.* (1 Jn 5:4)

We refuse to come into agreement with darkness and live from "lack." In Christ we are more than conquerors. We are in charge! When we get this faith/perception thing figured out we get to walk in amazing triumph over the shortages of this fallen world.

Living in "Favor"

Lori and I have noticed a trend that we experience regularly. We call it the "Favor Anointing." It began to catch our attention a couple of years ago when we were enjoying a get-away on our anniversary in a little town that has woven its way into our hearts over the years. It's a small gem in the Cascade Mountains called Leavenworth, a village with a Bavarian theme made up of a main street lined with quaint shops and eateries.

We were staying for a couple of nights at a B and B and decided to do some shopping on the first morning of our stay. We picked a shop to go in. We noticed it was empty at our arrival, but within a few minutes it was full of shoppers. We didn't think too much of it until we saw this pattern repeat itself too many times to be a coincidence. Over and over again, wherever we would go we marveled at the same outcome.

We noticed the same pattern when we were at a mall in Lacey, Washington. We were out shopping with our daughter Destiny and her "good" friend Robby. The same thing happened a variety of times to the four of us as we drifted from shop to shop. We would go into an empty store and watch it fill with people in seconds following our entrance.

Just the other day Lori and I were in Portland, Oregon at a large shoe store. As we entered it was like a ghost town, and this was a big store. By the time we headed for the checkout counter there must have been nearly 80 people shopping for shoes.

I think we underestimate the influence we have in any given moment at any given place. Not only is there an amazing reality inside of those who believe, but there is an amazing deposit in the wake of believers. There is truly something that accompanies those who walk in the full understanding of their birthright in Jesus.

In the Gospel of Mark 16:17 the words of Jesus are highlighted as saying: *these signs will follow or accompany those who believe.* The word "signs" here means supernatural indicators. As believers we carry a supernatural environment of favor that is designed to influence. It is God's heart that we leak out His goodness wherever we go. How cool is that? By just being somewhere we can release Heaven to earth. Just by walking into a store the King is there to release His fragrance. It's like a magnet. People are drawn to His presence and usually don't even know it. Imagine when the Body of Christ gets a hold of this truth and begins to live ever day intentionally.

Jeff and Amy (one of our amazing young couples who know their identity) model this reality constantly. They live in "favor land" wherever they go and in whatever they do. The other day they were in one of our local restaurants having some together time as well as sharing an enormous cinnamon roll, when an elderly gentleman with cane in hand walked slowly by their table as he was exiting the establishment. A physical need is always one of our codes for action time. They both knew that this gentleman was now their assignment and quickly yet politely asked him if they could pray for him. Half expecting a "no" to their request because he was leaving and because of the crowded public setting, they were pleased to receive an enthusiastic "yes." They gently laid their hands on the man and said a very brief prayer of blessing and healing, and the man was on his way. Although not seeing anything transpire visibly, Jeff and Amy were happy to be available to release God's goodness at a moment's notice. In a matter of minutes they were surprised to see the elderly gentleman come back to their table with the manager of the restaurant saying, "Right there, those two…I want to pay for their meal. They prayed for me and I felt something in my body I've never felt before."

The man insisted on paying for their dessert and went on about what it meant for them to pray for him. Even though the contact with the man lasted no more than thirty seconds, the favor of God that Jeff and Amy carry was instantly released to that gentleman and shifted something in his life and in the atmosphere of that restaurant.

Speaking of favor…

Check out this next story as we hear more from the "Shop Girls":

Let me give you some background on these two amazing world changers. A few years ago they were in a business partnership with another friend, but things began to unravel as the revelation of their identity began to transform Kerry and Kelli's world. Before long the working arrangement between the three of them disintegrated amidst some hurt feelings, forcing a change which led to the "shop girls" new shop. In the course of this relationally painful season, one of the suppliers that the three of them had been working with turned her back on Kerry and Kelli; no longer offering them her services.

Here is one of Kerry's latest updates as she keeps me current with her "power culture" journey:

> TODAY I had yet another encounter. I have been working out with a personal trainer for about 6 weeks. His name is Greg and he is amazing. I see the light on him in my built-in viewfinder that "Happy" has gifted me with. About 3 weeks ago I was on my way to train and I prayed, "Ok, God. Open the door so that Brian can see you." When I arrived at the gym, I saw a gal there that came against Kelli and me when we were asked to leave because we prayed for people at the other shop. She was my rep for

my beauty products. She sided with my ex-business partner and decided to disengage from Kelli and me and no longer rep for our company. So there she was across the room and she spots me and immediately comes over to me and says "My shoulder is killing me, I can hardly take it anymore. I am in so much pain." So my normal response to such a need is "Be healed." She stops; looks at me with wild eyes (because she is shocked that I would speak that out in public—the very thing I was asked to leave my job over) and says, "What did you say?" I said, "Be healed in Jesus' name."

She thinks about it for a second and says, "Well that would be nice," so I say, "Put your shoulder over here let me touch it." So she does and she is immediately healed. She was so excited she started pumping it up and down and all around with total amazement all over her face. So I get up from my workout and go across to my trainer and say, "Hey Greg, see that girl over there? She just got healed." Greg says, "How do you know?" I said, "Because I prayed for her and look at her. Jesus healed her." He was watching her pumping her arm up and down wildly. A week later she calls me at work (remember, she hadn't spoken to me or called on my company in over a year). She says to me, "Kerry it's a total miracle, it is totally healed." Then she says, "Tell Kelli that I will be in to your business to call on you guys in a week." By the way, when she arrived she brought me over $200 worth of free product. . . That doesn't ever happen with the reps! Also, when she showed up she told us that the injury that was healed was a torn rotator cuff that had been torn for 3 years.

So today, I said on the way to see my trainer, "God open the door a little wider for Greg to see you." So when I got there, we were training and this guy walks up to Greg and me and says, "I'm having an off day today. My workout isn't good." And I say, "I declare a good workout for you today. Then he proceeds to tell me that his shoulder is all messed up and he cannot lift weights. So immediately I lay my hand on his shoulder and declare healing and he gets healed right in front of Greg's eyes. He's now having an amazing day and God is in a good mood and everyone is getting touched by his good mood. Brian saw God today. He is totally hammered in a good way and he knows it. I prayed for his ankle (Greg's) and I declared it whole. He was too afraid to try it and test it out, so I declared that he is worthy of being healed, which shocked him because I read his mail and I told him to call me when he realized it was a done deal. I'll let you know when he calls. Yaaaaaa, Go Daddy!

p.s. love you lots, Kerry —- one of many stories happening on a daily basis.

And the next week I got "THE REST OF THE STORY" as Kerry e-mails me with another update...

> Hi Pastor Scott, I have more to the miracle situation with my trainer Greg. Yesterday, first of all three people were healed. The first one which took place at our shop was my very first customer. She was born and raised a Baptist missionary's daughter. Her thumb was healed. This was the first miracle she had ever seen, and also the first time God had ever touched her. The 2nd miracle was the 3rd customer of the day, Heidi. She has had multiple healings in our shop. She came and expected one. Her knee was totally healed. She cried & cried. She is amazing. . The 3rd miracle: I was headed to the gym after work. Greg spots me as soon as I get there and runs over to me. The gym is packed. He says, "Hurry Kerry, Sandi needs a healing. Her shoulder is all messed up." By the way, Sandi is my good friend. So— right before Greg's eyes, God heals Sandi in the middle of the gym. She's so happy. Greg is jumping up and down and totally excited.
>
> So moving on to today. . .I get to the gym for my training session. As I'm on my way I say to God, "God open the door a little wider for Greg to see you." I get there. Greg (with his ankle issue) says, "Kerry, my ankle & hip are killing me today." I say, "Greg, you know God is going to

heal that." He says, "I'm scared that he might not want to."

I say, "He does, please let me pray for it." He got healed today, Pastor Scott. All the way! I knew he was going to. . .YAAAAAAAA! I love being his favorite!

Have a great day.

Kerry, p.s. I love you lots. . .

Come on, how good is that? This is the Kingdom in operation, released through people who are not struggling with "being" amazing so they in turn can "do" amazing.

The Personalization of His Magnificence

In most traditional church worship services it is a fairly common and appropriate practice to give glory, adoration and praise to God—magnifying the Lord Jesus and expressing a rock solid conviction of His divine ability and power over any force of darkness and His supremacy over all things. "Our God reigns!" The very sound of those words makes you want to join in and echo the sentiments.

What is not so common in the average church is our personal connection to that declaration. It seems to be a normal response to acknowledge God's greatness yet awkward to even consider that God's greatness transfers us to a place of prominence. Somehow we have fallen into a trap of a fear of pride to the degree that we can't embrace the reality of our Heavenly status as sons and daughters of our Heavenly Father. Why does our status as "amazing" in Him seem to throw some people off?

A fear of failure comes from a perception of lack. If I lack then I expect to fail; therefore I can't be amazing. If we view ourselves as anything less than amazing it's because we don't understand what God's grace gift has done inside of us.

In a personal lack culture we can never break the power of being afraid of the influence of the world. Instead of being a confident influencer we will live in fear of the evils of this world.

Markus is one of our amazing young guys in our Promise Family. He's twelve, and he knows who he is and he knows that his light is more powerful than darkness. One day he had a neighbor friend over who was about half his age. This neighbor friend had been raised in moral poverty and Markus was very aware of it. Knowing that the kind of actions and language this boy was used to exhibiting were not acceptable in his home, Markus took him aside and began to release his culture into the young boy, saying to him, "We both know how amazing you are and we're going to show my mom how amazing you are." Instead of being afraid of the influence of the boy's darkness, Markus was pulling the boy into his light. Instead of isolating to keep from having someone else's darkness rub off, Markus was embracing an opportunity to advance the Kingdom. Markus's parents had built a confidence and a mindset into their son that is the core of being a "world changer." Markus is not afraid of being amazing or fearful of the contagions of the darkness in others.

Having this inner confidence instilled at an early age in no way influences a young person like Markus to manifest some weird sense of pride. I have found the opposite of pride to be true for those who embrace their heavenly status in Jesus. When you realize you have nothing to do with it, that it's totally a gift, it nurtures a heart of gratitude, humility and honor.

The other day our one-year-old grandson Rais, had a bad cold and could hardly breathe. His lungs were congested, and his sinuses were plugged up. Casey and Ashley recognized it as an opportunity to instill into Rais's big brother Laik, now two, a power culture. Having Laik repeat a simple prayer over Rais's body as they helped Laik lay hands on his brother, they finished praying and thanked Jesus for healing Rais's condition. They stood back and marveled as Rais's lungs and sinuses instantly cleared, leaving no trace of a cold.

At The Promise we promote a culture that goes beyond theory and teaching. It's a culture that hits you in the heart and transforms your reality and breaks off the limitations of the world we live in. It's a reality that defies logic and transcends age limitations. In Christ it's who we are and it's what we're supposed to do.

Rhema Code Truth: To live effectively in a power culture we can't be afraid of being powerful. It's who we are.

A few concluding thoughts...

This was God's whisper to me, summarizing what's at the center of His purpose in leading people:

The legacy of a successful ministry is what transpires on the inside of those who follow or are influenced by any leader. It's not measuring success by how many we can gather but by raising up supernatural World Changers who live beyond natural limitations as they resource their lives from the place of a completely transformed identity. It's the radical transformation of a heart and mind that distinctly and consistently reflects God's supernatural reality in a fallen world.

The revelation of our identity shift "in Christ" is such a powerful truth! It's a *Rhema* that God is casting on the Church at this moment and it will revolutionize the Bride.

Is there anything that compares to the Divine touch on a human Heart—when Glory intercepts faith like the blending of precious ingredients making up an amazing new creation? I don't think so!

The Rhema Code is a "Reality" with world changing ability. It is a spiritual DNA shift of endless possibilities and culture changing dynamics; an equipping and empowering of individuals with Supernatural identity and power.

As the core of this truth penetrates your heart you will never be the same. You won't see things the same, you won't hear things the same, you won't think the same and you won't act and talk the same!

As you learn to agree with Papa, I pray you will

"BE". . ."*AMP*'d":
Amazing! Miraculous! Perfect!

**Watch out world! "Here comes the Bride!"
Spotless and powerful!**

You rose from the grave restored my life
Set fire to the sky and washed me white
Your love is a blanket that covers me
You give me wings and set me free
……..

Grab hold of my soul take over
Saturate my heart and use me
Let your kingdom reign on me
Pour out your passion consume me
……..

My life is not my own

I lay it down to you alone

Your love overwhelms my soul

It gives me life and now I'm yours again

— "Now I'm Yours" by Casey Schang

CHAPTER NINE

The Cost of the Code

Is there any price too high to pay for the authentic reality of God "to you, in you and through you?" To experience His presence in such a real way that you can feel Him, sense Him and be smothered in His love and goodness? I don't think so! Not even the price of rejection, misunderstanding, loss of respect and admiration is too great. Nor is the loss of recognition, position, influence, affluence or affirmation. There is no price too high to pay!

On the scale of value, God is gold! Neither the praises of man nor the fear of man compare to the vise grip He will place on your heart if you let Him. If you choose Him over all other things, you will pay the price but you will pay it gladly. You may be misunderstood but you will be in good company.

Has there ever been anyone more misunderstood, rejected or neglected than Jesus? In whatever form God has come on the scene in human history—whether in Spirit or in bodily form He never failed to knock the scales of "normal" off the table. He never tries to accommodate the natural mind when He manifests Himself. He is in a constant mode of violating the natural senses of human beings. He never allows Himself to be defined logically or through a natural lens. Remarkably, He never shifts His approach to our hearts in the face of rejection. Whether we choose to walk into Him or away from Him, He remains steadfast in His "all or nothing" offer.

God has given us an open invitation into His world through Jesus and the offer of eternal life was never prefaced with our inviting Him into "our" world. The idea of inviting Jesus "into" our heart can be a bit misleading, and a bit of an understatement, compared to His intention in the deal. When inner transformation takes place in a life, it's no longer life "status quo." He doesn't burst onto the scene of our heart to simply comfort us. He sends the comforter because He knows the journey will be so radical that we will need Holy Spirit comforting.

Our daughter, Destiny, is one of my heroes. She is as nice and kind as a person could be yet she has epitomized counting the cost. Her journey has led her to regularly be among people who are not "churched" people and her unwavering authentic representation of Jesus always creates a knife-like atmosphere from those who live in darkness. Either they love her or they hate her, or at best tolerate her. It would have been easy for her to compromise her passion for Jesus just to make life a little easier—just to fit in. But the benefits of leaping into His Kingdom do not include anything to do with popularity or social status. I mean when you take His offer "hook, line and sinker," your world becomes His world and the similarities between His world and this natural one polarize at the point of "decent and in order!"

God is so unpredictable that He becomes predictable. We can actually predict that we never know what He's going to do next in our lives.

I've used this phrase many times when describing what my job description entails at The Promise: "I lead a crazy church; crazy good that is!" I tell folks that it's not for the faint of heart, but if they will stick around long enough I guarantee it will change their lives.

As a leader there is no way to release the reality of God in a context that will be soothing and comforting to a person who chooses to make their "God application" fit into a natural grid. He's the "Wild God" and he doesn't harness well! Simply put: God redefines for us what is normal and what is orderly.

Rhema Code Truth: God is the "Wild God" and He doesn't harness well!

My heart really does go out to those who are seeking a real dose of God through a grid of logic. It can be quite disconcerting for some to surrender their misconceptions of what God is supposed to look like at any given moment of Holy Spirit manifestation; especially when you consider that He usually manifests in some way, shape or form through people. What a conflict that can bring—religious resolve versus God expressing Himself through people…wow!

The church at large lives in such a state of fear of being deceived as it is that it magnifies the irony of the situation: leaders trying hard to keep things under control while promoting God! Now that is a serious conflict of interests. When you follow the life of Jesus in the New Testament, He breaks every mold of "order" to the point of being crucified. I am not a proponent of disorder. I am; however, a proponent of God's "order."

I have been asked a variety of times by leaders if our paradigm "shift" at The Promise has cost us people. What I want to tell them is that that's the wrong question. We place a premium on knowing God and being in His presence. This is such a core value that we are more concerned about missing Him than we are about "losing people." It's never our goal to lose people but it's not our goal to keep people. It's our goal to transform people.

God's expressed core value of shifting humanity's focus from this fallen realm to His heavenly one is what drives our ministry engine. Jesus expressed this value clearly when He taught in the synagogue in Capernaum following His miraculous feeding of the 5000 in the sixth chapter of John's Gospel. He wasn't the least bit driven by drawing a crowd or escalating church attendance when He told the crowd that He was offering His flesh and blood as a meal for those who were desiring eternal life. He was, however, very interested in escalating people's awareness of a superior Kingdom. His focus was not on teaching the people things that fit into their grid. His intent was to deliver them from their grid. This may have cost Him some followers in the short run but He wasn't keying in on ordinary followers. He was keying in on World Changers who understood what it meant to live from an eternal condition and perspective.

Following His teaching in chapter six, He asked His disciples if they too wanted to walk away from Him like all of the rest had, and Peter answered Jesus with this statement, "Lord to whom shall we go? You have the words of eternal life."

The words of eternal life—did you hear that? What does that mean? Well I know what it doesn't mean. It has nothing to do with a soothing message that appeases people's consciences; and "words of life" in God's context certainly aren't limited to a solution to mankind's sin problem or a rite of passage to heaven. The "words of life" are the words that break the power of limited thinking and temporal resourcing—words that eliminate the idea of impossible!

I remember the time I heard a prominent leader tell a large group at a conference that building a doctrine around Jesus walking on the water wouldn't be something he would advise.

I've thought about that statement many times since that day some years ago, and I've come to a conclusion. I think we need "water walking" as a doctrine, and I think Jesus was building a doctrine when He walked on the water. Look at the progression: He miraculously feeds five thousand people; He walks on water; and He offers His flesh and blood to a bunch of religious people. Is there a pattern here? Of course there is! It's the pattern we see all through His life once He stepped into His ministry of destroying the domain of darkness. Jesus lived in radical opposition to a fallen world system and how people viewed His methods was irrelevant to Him. He was the door to a new way of thinking and the old way wasn't going to shift easily. There were enemies to be made and people to offend. That's just the reality of it!

There is a price to pay but the investment is so worth it: radically transformed people who "get it," people who have their eyes opened to the extreme opposite of the degree Adam and Eve had theirs closed; the eye of the Spirit restored to humanity. That's our quest—not some religious experience or elevated church attendance, but true blue believers, authentic followers consumed by Jesus and passionately living life from His world.

I've been asked to comment on "priorities" a variety of times over the years and what people usually have in mind when asking about priorities is along this line:

Put God first. . .
Family second. . .
Church third. . .
Job fourth. . .

The last two go back and forth depending on who you talk to. If you ask a Pastor he may put church higher up the list, and may even call that as putting God first. If you ask the average person to be honest with their answer according to the time and energy they invest, the fourth one would probably be the first one. But it's all a moot point.

My answer to prioritizing life is: the moment you consider where to put God on your priority list you are sorely missing the Heart of God. We can't prioritize God! God is not a priority. He is our life. We can't fit Him in. We are in Him. In Him we live and move and have our being. In the Kingdom we don't "do church" and we don't "do God."

Many times I've told my church family, "This is not heaven, but while we are here we are going to live from heaven," knowing that at times it may not be convenient for the moment or popular, yet it is still the best way to live—His way. "His Kingdom come, His will be done, on Earth as it is in Heaven"—to me, in me, and through me. No matter what we go through or how long we go through it, it is immeasurable compared to eternity. Short term sacrifice for long term gain; no problem, for there is really no sacrifice in the Kingdom. When you have your eye of the Spirit opened by His amazing touch of love and you see things from His world, everything changes. That's what Jesus was banking on and He never lives in deficit!

Every chance I get I look at my church family and never stop being deeply moved. What incredible people I have the joy and privilege of loving and living with in this fantastic Kingdom journey.

This may not be the most popular statement, but it is one of the most powerful statements: In Christ you are perfect! If you believe—I mean the "believe" He's talking about—well, that puts you in the "amazing" category. Now your journey is to grow into that reality as the eyes of your understanding are enlightened. Now let's go change the world!

THE RHEMA CODE

Rhema Code Truth: If you don't know who you are, no one else will either!

Rhema Code Truth: God's design for your life is one of supernatural influence now!

Rhema Code Truth: In Christ, you are offered a literal brand new start—a new birth with a new everything attached to it!

Rhema Code Truth: Authentic inner transformation is not a theory, it's not a hope, it's not a teaching—it's a world changing reality.

[handwritten annotations: OPENING: The Information you are about to hear is (a) ? marks (b) I maybe -- no (c) see blackboard white board / It is -- a world and a reality waiting for you / empowering]

Rhema Code Truth: In our walk with God we cannot afford to put "doing" in front of "being."

Rhema Code Truth: Our love for Jesus must have a tighter grip on our hearts than the voices and faces around us!

[handwritten: Good Graphic to portray]

Rhema Code Truth: The fear of losing people can't override the passion to empower people.

Rhema Code Truth: Intimacy is the birthing of our identity in Christ.

Rhema Code Truth: By virtue of a new bloodline you "are" amazing and powerful.

Rhema Code Truth: In Christ we no longer live in a condition of depravity and no longer have a fallen nature—erasing "lack" from our vocabulary.

Rhema Code Truth: Living in a "from" paradigm is an "inside" job.

Rhema Code Truth: Living "from" the inside out is priority for successful Kingdom advancement.

Rhema Code Truth: In the New Testament era, we are the "Holy of Holies." We are the habitation of God's presence. We no longer have to go through a variety of steps to get to God—we host God!

Rhema Code Truth: To make any attempt at applying any of the virtues of the Kingdom through a mindset of a fallen grid apart from grace and the complete work of the cross will only lead to human effort attempting to work out Heavenly 'ideas.'

Rhema Code Truth: "Believing" is measured by where you think from and how that affects your actions and attitudes.

Rhema Code Truth: Because of what Jesus has accomplished inside of us, we are able to "live from" complete rather that "live toward" complete.

Rhema Code Truth: Our perception of what we are on the inside is what we will display on the outside.

Rhema Code Truth: Living from a lack perception will place a burden on all things around us to become part of the solution for our state of "incomplete."

Rhema Code Truth. Only Jesus holds the key to your heart; allowing anyone else to "complete" you will only end in disappointment!

Rhema Code Truth (Relationship Success Key): Your ability to enjoy and flourish in loving, quality relationships is directly connected to your personal understanding and "yieldedness" to the complete work of Christ within you.

Rhema Code Truth: Complete is a state of being—a "condition" that we learn to live "from" as we walk in the revelation of how amazing God is and how amazing He has made us.

Rhema Code Truth: That which we live "from vs. towards" defines us.

Rhema Code Truth: When the Church devalues the completeness of spiritual conception, the world will devalue the completeness of natural conception!

Rhema Code Truth: Social reform will be inspired by a theological reform of the "complete" work of grace in the heart of man.

Rhema Code Truth: When we devalue the power of conception, so does the world!

Rhema Code Truth: Your ability to flourish supernaturally is directly connected to your perception of how God views you.

Rhema Code Truth: Obedience is not an activity; it's a condition of agreement with God's heart that launches us into activity.

Rhema Code Truth: A person can keep all the rules and be in open rebellion toward God.

Rhema Code Truth: Lack thinking is identifying yourself from an old man paradigm.

Rhema Code Truth: Faith = Perception

Rhema Code Truth: It is imperative that we make the unseen realm more influential than that which we can see!

Rhema Code Truth: Only "higher perception" and "intentional living" will advance the Kingdom.

Rhema Code Truth: The conflict of paradigms is a war of "natures."

Rhema Code Truth: Jesus is not an antibiotic for your sins. He pronounces a death sentence to your sin nature. He puts to death the sin issue in your heart.

Rhema Code Truth: The leverage of the accuser was broken at Calvary. It was the end of one era and the beginning of another.

Rhema Code Truth: Jesus is not coming back for a Bride with an identity crisis and His bride is not dirty or ugly.

Rhema Code Truth: A Law Keeper is a Law Breaker.

Rhema Code Truth: One with God is a majority.

Rhema Code Truth: When you start to personalize your role in advancing the Kingdom, something happens on the inside, something begins to shift.

Rhema Code Truth: God will do what seems impossible and He will do it through us.

Rhema Code Truth: Love is only tested when things get testy.

Rhema Code Truth: We choose to live in and from an "Empowering Culture" instead of a "gathering culture."

Rhema Code Truth: When our eyes are opened to the revelation of our supernatural status in Christ, a whole new world of exciting manifestations of God's miraculous power becomes a reality.

Rhema Code Truth: Learning to yield to His presence is the launching pad of power.

Rhema Code Truth: To live effectively in a power culture we can't be afraid of being powerful. It's who we are.

Rhema Code Truth: God is the "Wild God" and He doesn't harness well!